T0299251

The Essentials of M&A Due Diligence

How can you be sure you are buying the company you think you are? Are you sure it is as good as the seller says? How can you be certain unexpected costs and obligations will not suddenly appear once you are the owner and responsible for them? How best can you arm yourself for the negotiations? Have you worked out precisely what you are going to do with it once it is yours? How do you set the priorities for change to recoup the premium you have paid for it?

The answer to all these questions, and many more, lies within a series of three comprehensive yet concise volumes by Peter Howson.

The Essentials of M&A Due Diligence, the first in the series, is a must for anyone who needs to master the essentials of due diligence with the minimum effort and in the minimum amount of time. Straightforward and unbiased, it sets out the fundamentals of pre-acquisition investigations, showing which are appropriate and why.

Peter Howson draws on thirty years of M&A and due diligence experience gained both in industry and as an adviser. His M&A experience began at the British conglomerate TI Group, where he was part of the small team which, through 75 acquisitions and disposals, transformed it from a UK focused supplier of commodity products into a global specialist engineering company. This was followed by a spell in Corporate Finance at the Investment Bank Barings, where he focused on domestic and cross-border deals in manufacturing industries. He continued his career with senior finance and M&A roles with British Steel and the automotive company T&N before spending 15 years as a London based commercial due diligence specialist advising corporates and private equity on potential acquisitions.

Routledge Focus on Economics and Finance

The fields of economics are constantly expanding and evolving. This growth presents challenges for readers trying to keep up with the latest important insights. Routledge Focus on Economics and Finance presents short books on the latest big topics, linking in with the most cutting-edge economics research.

Individually, each title in the series provides coverage of a key academic topic, whilst collectively the series forms a comprehensive collection across the whole spectrum of economics.

For a full list of titles in this series, please visit www.routledge.com/Routledge-Focus-on-Economics-and-Finance/book-series/RFEF

The Essentials of M&A Due Diligence

Peter Howson

Routledge
Taylor & Francis Group

LONDON AND NEW YORK

First published 2018
by Routledge
2 Park Square, Milton Park, Abingdon, Oxon OX14 4RN

and by Routledge
711 Third Avenue, New York, NY 10017

Routledge is an imprint of the Taylor & Francis Group, an informa business

© 2018 Peter Howson

British Library Cataloguing-in-Publication Data
A catalogue record for this book is available from the British
Library

Library of Congress Cataloging-in-Publication Data
A catalog record for this book has been requested

ISBN: 978-1-138-09304-1 (hbk)
ISBN: 978-1-315-10709-7 (ebk)

Typeset in Times New Roman
by Apex CoVantage, LLC

Contents

vi *Contents*

Illustrations

Figures

Tables

1   Introduction

Due diligence is the process of finding out about what you are buying. It is often criticised as a way of spending a lot of money to tell you what you already know – which is exactly what it should do, preferably without costing too much.

Due diligence comes just before the final negotiations. By then sellers have nothing to gain by giving a buyer time to probe and find reasons to chip away at the agreed price. This means the buyer has a short time to collect and digest a lot of information, often with imperfect access. Without building up a prior body of knowledge on the target, sufficient to highlight the 'known unknowns', a buyer puts itself at a disadvantage.

After that, it is all about project management. The last thing a buyer needs is expensive advisers doing their own thing or falling over each other. Focus is key. This book is about helping to decide what information is and where and how to get it so making due diligence manageable and cost effective. And if it only confirms what you already know, so what?

When is it done?

Acquisitions come about in different ways, from long courtships with lots of goodwill built up on both sides to controlled auctions where a buyer hardly gets a look in before the final stages. At some point towards the end will come Heads of Terms/Heads of Agreement/A Letter of Intent. Whatever called, it is a (non-binding) document which sets out the main points agreed (price, timing, etc.) and the basis on which the two sides are prepared to proceed. It confirms that the parties are serious and signals that (formal) due diligence can begin. Until then, the buyer will have relied on public information, information released to help the transaction – an information memorandum, partial access to a data room, vendor due diligence and maybe even management discussions – but has not yet had the opportunity systematically to research the workings of the target and verify the accuracy of the data it has been given.

Why do it?

It is possible to buy a company without doing any due diligence; it is not a legal requirement in acquisitions, so why bother? What persuades the sceptical CEO to spend money verifying what management has already told him?

First of all, without making the enquiries you will not know where the risks are, meaning that you can only negotiate standard warranties. There is nothing wrong with that if the deal is small and/or the buyer's knowledge of the target is very good.

Second, due diligence can unearth problems no-one really knew existed. Sellers, usually quite genuinely, believe their companies to be problem-free. Often they will have lived with what outsiders would see as 'problems' without any harmful effects.

Another benefit of due diligence is avoiding litigation. Litigation is expensive and uncertain. Comparatively speaking, due diligence is cheap. Buyers should be much more comfortable knowing about problems beforehand, rather than being left with the possibility of making warranty or indemnity claims or having to sue the seller.

Third, knowledge is power. Due diligence gives the buyer knowledge. The more that is known about a seller's business, the better the buyer is equipped for the negotiations which lie ahead.

Fourth, as a defence against charges of negligence in a transaction. The US courts, for example, have found that it is not reasonable to rely exclusively on the target's management. What they tell you must be double-checked through an independent investigation.

Once completed, due diligence findings feed into the final negotiations by identifying risks against which the buyer should negotiate some sort of protection or guarantee with the seller.

Last and by no means least, due diligence should have an important part to play in the acquisition making a decent return. A buyer will always pay more for a business than a seller thinks it is worth. To make a return on the transaction, a buyer must either know more than the seller does or be able to do more with the business than the seller can. Due diligence findings should therefore also assess the strategic rationale of the deal, the business's standalone value and growth prospects and the size, timing and achievability of synergies. Findings should feed into the post-acquisition integration plan.

Under English law, the principle of '*caveat emptor*' or 'buyer beware' means that virtually no terms are implied in favour of a purchaser of shares in a company. Consequently, protection must be dealt with by express contractual provision. The usual form of protection is through warranties and indemnities, but a purchaser should use all means of protection available:

due diligence, warranties, indemnities, reductions in the purchase price, retentions from the purchase price, earn outs, guarantees, insurance, the exclusion of certain assets and remedial work at the seller's cost.

Warranties

A warranty is, in effect, a 'guarantee' by the seller that a certain state of affairs exists. Warranties are statements of fact which the seller confirms to be true. An example might be that the target company is not involved in any litigation. If the seller knows that this is not true, it discloses the real facts (e.g. the details of the actual litigation) in a disclosure letter. By disclosing exceptions to the warranties, the seller will have no liability for the matters disclosed. If a buyer tries to claim for one of these items, the seller can hold its hands up and say, 'but I told you about that'.

Warranties have two functions as far as a purchaser is concerned. The first is that the disclosure letter usually contains a lot of useful information about the target. It may even flag up liabilities which were previously unknown, in which case the purchaser may try to negotiate a price adjustment. The second is contractual. Any breach of the guarantee given by the warranties which has a bearing on the value of the target entitles the purchaser to a retrospective price adjustment. That is to say, where there is a breach of warranty, a buyer who can prove loss is entitled to damages to put itself back in the position it would have been in had the warranty been true.

Great, except that there are problems in relying on warranties. It can be difficult (and costly) to prove that there has been a breach, that there has been a loss resulting from the breach and how much less the target company is worth as a result of that loss – especially several years down the line, when all sorts of other things have changed, too.

Indemnities

An indemnity is a guaranteed remedy against a specific liability. The buyer is entitled to it regardless of whether or not the value of the target is affected or whether the liability was disclosed in the disclosure letter.

Indemnities enable the purchaser to adopt a 'wait and see' policy, especially if there is uncertainty about the size of the liability and/or whether it will crystallise. The sale and purchase agreement can provide that if the liability crystallises, the purchaser will be compensated an amount to cover the loss suffered. One of the most common indemnities is an indemnity against tax liabilities. Here the vendor promises to meet a liability should it arise.

The value of an indemnity (or a warranty, for that matter) depends on the financial worth of the seller. If the seller is not particularly creditworthy or, for example, has moved its assets to an offshore jurisdiction or into his wife's name, some security may be called for. This could take the form of a deposit of funds in an escrow account, a third party guarantee or even retention from the purchase price for a stipulated period after completion.

Like warranties, difficulties of proof may make indemnities difficult to rely on. They may also be time limited and financially capped.

The different due diligence disciplines

There are a number of different types of due diligence which can be carried out. Table 1.1 summarises the three main areas, while Table 1.2 shows the other usual due diligence topics. It looks like a forbidding list. In any deal, some of these will be more important than others. Some will be carried out as topics in their own right, and others subsumed under other headings. For example, human resources, IPR and property could be covered by legal due diligence; tax, insurance, IT, operational and pension by financial due diligence and management and technical by commercial due diligence.

All the above, except property and operational, are covered in later chapters. Property is covered under legal, while operational is so highly tailored to the target company it is difficult to generalise about it much beyond what is said in Table 1.2 and in the appropriate headings in the chapter on financial due diligence.

Table 1.1 The main due diligence topics

Due diligence topic	Focus of enquiries	Results sought
• Financial	• Validation of historical financial information, review of management and systems.	• Confirm underlying profit, provide a basis for valuation, determine cash free/debt free adjustments.
• Legal	• Verification of assets, confirmation of title, contractual agreements, problem-spotting.	• Priorities for warranties and indemnities and other means of legal protection, validation of existing contracts, drafting of sale and purchase agreement.
• Commercial	• Market dynamics, target's competitive position, target's commercial prospects.	• Sustainability of future profits, formulation of strategy for the combined business, input to valuation.

Table 1.2 The other due diligence disciplines

Due diligence topic	Focus of enquiries	Results sought
• Human resources and culture	• Makeup of the workforce, terms and conditions of employment, level of commitment and motivation, organisational culture.	• Uncovering any employment liabilities, assessing the potential human resources costs and risks, prioritising HR integration issues, assessing cultural fit, costing and planning the post-deal HR changes.
• Management	• Management quality, organisational structure.	• Identification of integration issues.
• Pension	• Various pension plans and plan valuations.	• Minimise the risks of under-funding.
• Tax	• Existing tax levels, liabilities and arrangements.	• Avoid any unforeseen tax liabilities, opportunities to optimise the tax position of the combined business.
• Environmental	• Liabilities arising from sites and processes, compliance with regulations.	• Potential liabilities, nature and cost of actions to limit them.
• IT	• Performance, ownership and adequacy of current systems.	• Cost and feasibility of integrating systems, cybersecurity, scope for improving the business through IT.
• Technical	• Performance, ownership and adequacy of technology.	• Value and sustainability of product technology.
• Operational	• Production techniques, validity of current technology.	• Technical threats, sustainability of current methods, opportunities for improvement, investment requirements.
• Intellectual property rights (IPRs)	• Validity, duration and protection of patents and other IPRs.	• Expiration, impact and cost.
• Property	• Deeds, land registry records and lease agreements.	• Confirmation of title, valuation and costs/potential of property assets.
• Anti-trust	• The various national filing requirements, some of which can be expensive if not complied with, degree of market/information sharing with competitors.	• Merger control filings and clearance, an assessment of any anti-trust risks posed by the target's activities, an assessment of the enforceability of the target's contracts.

Different types of due diligence

As well as different due diligence disciplines, there are also different types. Most of this book is concerned with the traditional, buyer commissioned due diligence prior to the purchase of a private company. There are other forms.

Vendor due diligence

Vendor due diligence (VDD) is due diligence commissioned by the owners of the business and given to prospective buyers, with the aim of giving them all the information they need to make a final bid. It is commissioned for a number of reasons, most, but not all, designed to control the information flow and so maintain negotiating advantage. As such, vendor due diligence:

• Stops management, advisers, customers and suppliers being deluged by questions
• Gets all the bad news out up front so discovery of problems later is not used as an excuse to chisel the price
• May be a device for hiding or 'spinning' problems

Buyers should be wary of due diligence reports presented by the seller. The tone of reports, if not the facts, can always be varied according to the brief. If given vendor due diligence, a buyer should read it and:

• Assess the reputation of the firm which carried out the work
• Read between the lines. What is not there that should be?
• Meet the firm(s) which produced the work (be very suspicious if the seller will not allow this) and ask for whatever clarification you need

Due diligence in public bids

Due diligence in public bids can be very different to private or semi-private transactions. With hostile bids, expect, at best, the minimum of co-operation. If a public bid is friendly, i.e. recommended by the target's board, some due diligence is possible – although given the price sensitivity, full, unfettered access is going to be a problem until the deal is announced. Where there are competitive bids, the target company has, by law, to supply the same information to the new bidder as it did to the original bidder. The slight get-out is that the second bidder cannot just ask for all the information supplied, but has to ask specific questions. Nevertheless, this can act as a constraint on due diligence in public bids, as it is not unknown for competitors to enter the fray on fishing expeditions. A target company may therefore not want to disclose sensitive information, even to a recommended bidder, just in case a competitor announces a bid and the information has to be handed over.

Due diligence in public offerings

Due diligence for an offering of securities is different than for an acquisition. The focus is on complete and reliable information on the target company so that underwriters do not misrepresent to potential buyers.

Due diligence when buying from the receiver

Receivers move quickly. This can severely limit what can be achieved by due diligence. If anything, due diligence is more important with receiverships than with normal acquisitions. The *quid pro quo* of compressed timescales is that the price is so low that a few transaction risks are worth taking. However, compared even with distressed prices, risks can be huge: there will be no warranty protection, there may be issues around title to stock or the costs of maintaining the goodwill of key suppliers and the truth is that businesses get into trouble for a reason. Understanding why a company is in receivership could be crucial not only to making an offer, but also to turning it round. Risk can be reduced by buying the business, rather than the company.

Conclusion

Due diligence has two objectives:

1   Reduce negotiation risk. A seller is bound to know far more about a business than a buyer. In Anglo-Saxon countries, *caveat emptor*, or buyer beware, is central to the whole acquisition process. Due diligence should therefore:

   • Verify that the buyer is buying what it thinks it is buying. This involves giving comfort on:

      • Current and future sales and profits
      • The size of assets and liabilities
      • Identifying points against which protection should be sought

2   Reduce deal risk. Acquisitions are risky; most fail. Implementation success and overall acquisition success are strongly correlated. Good due diligence is structured so that it informs the post-acquisition planning, which really means helping achieve the required pay back

2   Getting started

Due diligence is a balancing act between cost and risk. It does not have to cover everything. Often there will be special areas of concern, some of which will have come out of the pre-deal investigations. It would be surprising if there were no legal or financial due diligence. Both are needed to get the deal done, but obsession with either to the detriment of other areas is not a good idea. After that, it depends on the rationale for the deal, as shown in Table 2.1.

There is no right answer to the question, 'what is enough due diligence?' In the end, it comes down to comfort. When you feel comfortable making a firm recommendation, supported by synergy papers and a fully costed list of post-acquisition actions, and you feel well placed to negotiate contractual protection, you can stand down the due diligence team.

Dealing with obstacles

The specific sources of information for each of the due diligence areas are covered in the following chapters. More generally, buyers should be sensitive to the stress on its own personnel and on its relationship with the seller:

- Due diligence is a major disruption
- In non–Anglo Saxon countries, it is often seen as a sign of mistrust by the seller
- Sellers will always be afraid of the consequences for the future of the business and/or its sale to someone else if the deal does not go ahead

Even with a perfect relationship between buyer and seller, there are a number of obstacles to contend with.

Confidentiality agreements

Due diligence relies heavily on information from the seller and on access to the target's management, facilities and advisers. Nothing is likely to

Table 2.1 The different types of M&A

M&A type	Strategic objectives	Due diligence emphasis
• Overcapacity	• Eliminate overcapacity, gain market share, achieve scale economies.	• Retention of market share, rationalisation costs – especially human resources and IT.
• Geographic roll-up	• Economies of scale while retaining a local service.	• Back office integration, customer retention, strength of local management
• Product or market extension	• Product line or geographic extension.	• Strength of product/market position relative to the competition.
• M&A as research and development (R&D)	• Acquisitions used to launch new products and/or quickly build market positions.	• Technical and intellectual property due diligence, retention of key people.
• Industry convergence	• A company bets that a new industry is emerging and tries to establish a position by culling resources from existing industries whose boundaries are eroding.	• Commercial due diligence, technical due diligence, retention of key staff.

happen until the prospective buyer and seller have agreed on confidentiality undertakings.

As a minimum, the seller will want such an agreement to require the purchaser and its advisers to:

* Keep all disclosed information confidential
* Take all reasonable steps to keep it safe and secure
* Disclose the information only to those employees and advisers who need it for the transaction
* Use the information only for assessing the prospective transaction
* Return all documents (including copies) at the seller's request or at the conclusion or termination of negotiations

Where buyer and seller are direct competitors, there may be further clauses through which the buyer promises not to solicit any of the target's customers or employees during negotiations and for some time after if the deal does not complete.

Negotiating confidentiality agreements adds delay to what is usually a tight timetable. Using a protracted fight over the terms of the confidentiality agreement to restrict due diligence is definitely in the seller's interest. As parties rarely go to law over breaches of confidentiality, it is better to sign them and get on with the due diligence than waste a disproportionate time quibbling.

Cross-border considerations

Many of the obstacles in M&A arise because of an inherent conflict between buyer and seller. The buyer wants to see and understand everything before being bound to a deal. The seller wants to give nothing away until the buyer is bound. These natural differences are often exaggerated in cross-border deals.

The technical issues in cross-border deals are usually quite straightforward, especially with good local advice. In addition, there is a general acceptance that where a deal is being done with an Anglo-Saxon, an Anglo-Saxon format can be used. The real difficulties arise from cultural issues. For example, European law imposes a duty of good faith on the seller. This is the complete opposite to the English doctrine of *caveat emptor*. Under the Napoleonic Code, the seller owes a duty to the buyer to disclose any fact which might have a bearing on the value of the target. Unless the process has been patiently explained, a European seller is bound to see the Anglo-Saxon wish for extensive due diligence and an exhaustive set of warranties as a sign of mistrust.

Sensitive information

For understandable reasons, the seller will often not reveal sensitive commercial information until the last possible minute. Sellers do not want to hand potential (or in many deals, existing) competitors information which could damage the business if the deal does not go ahead. Unfortunately, late disclosure may lead to last minute negotiations, especially if the information turns out to be different from what the buyer had expected.

Restricted access to the seller's employees

Site visits are important means of collecting due diligence information. From the seller's perspective, it is natural to want to keep the proposed sale from employees. However, a seller should provide reasonable access to key personnel, and it is worth pushing hard for proper access. Not only are top management interviews are an essential part of the process, they often prove more willing than the seller to disclose matters that the purchaser should know about.

No access to customers

It is absolutely reasonable for a vendor to wish to protect the confidentiality of the discussions; indeed, it is in the acquirer's own interest to avoid any rumours in the market which may harm the target's relationships with its customers. What is not reasonable is for the vendor to seek to prevent a would-be acquirer in exclusive negotiations from talking on a confidential or undisclosed basis to customers. These are the people who know the real strengths and weaknesses of the company, its technology and its products.

Restricted timetables

The more time a buyer has, the greater the chance of it finding something it does not like. Most timetable issues are moveable and, indeed, by the time the discussions get round to due diligence timetables, the seller is so close to a deal that it would be foolish to alienate a prospective purchaser.

Most advisers will need at least three weeks to carry out their work, and more if they come across unexpected issues. Add time to brief them and to digest their findings at the end, and due diligence needs six weeks at the absolute minimum. If the seller will not budge on the timetable, try to negotiate a break fee. At least then due diligence costs will not be wasted if the work is not completed in time.

If the timetable is genuinely not moveable and only a limited due diligence exercise is possible, the purchaser should cover key issues and then take other precautionary steps to protect itself, e.g. ensuring that the warranties and indemnities are appropriately wide or by negotiating a retention of the purchase price to cover potential warranty claims. A seller that has restricted the would-be acquirer's due diligence programme is in a weak negotiating position if it tries to restrict warranties and indemnities as well.

Seeing the wood for the trees

A common due diligence problem is sheer volume of material available during the process, leading to useful information becoming concealed in irrelevant or unfocused data.

Data rooms

There is an art to dealing with the straightjacket that data rooms attempt to impose which is beyond the scope of this book. The objective of a data room is to give potential purchasers enough information for them to submit indicative bids. It is in the seller's interests to put in as much non-sensitive information as possible, and especially all the problems. If a seller gets all the problems out at the beginning while there are several interested parties, it leaves itself much less vulnerable to purchasers chipping the price. Bidders who make it through to the next round will usually have access to the more confidential or sensitive information and will be allowed to conduct normal due diligence.

Misrepresentation

Not all sellers, or their advisers, tell the whole truth all of the time. In the UK, it is a criminal offence if someone knowingly makes a false statement, promise or forecast to induce another person to enter into an agreement.

However, respondents can be misleading without deliberately lying. This can happen for perfectly innocent reasons; for example, they can get facts confused or try to hide the fact that they are not as knowledgeable as they should be. The due diligence practitioner, whatever the discipline, should always:

- Bear in mind that the nature of information impacts on its reliability:
  - Internal information is usually more reliable than external
  - How and from whom it is obtained can be important
  - More reliance can be placed on information that is independently verifiable
- Be on the lookout for inconsistencies that are material
- Ask open ended questions in interviews
- Remember that past behaviour can be a good predictor of future behaviour

Much of the really useful information will come from interviews. Where these are face to face, say with target management, it is always useful to have two interviewers. One is there to ask the questions; the other is there to listen and watch. Body language can say a lot.

How much information is verified is going to be largely based on the buyer's or due diligence investigator's opinion of the source of the information. As a rough guide, the following will always require verification:

- Information that is not publicly available
- Any details of future contracted business
- The existence of physical assets
- Product warranties
- The background of directors and senior staff
- Anything which does not seem believable

Dealing with the shortcomings of due diligence

The fairest and probably most sensible way of apportioning liabilities is to make the seller liable for everything pre-completion and the buyer for everything post-completion. Trying to achieve this happy equilibrium cannot be achieved through due diligence alone. However, thorough the due diligence may be, it is not a substitute for legal protection in the contract (and vice-versa). Due diligence and warranties and indemnities should be seen as separate weapons:

- Due diligence cannot uncover or quantify the size and likelihood of every acquisition risk. Legal protection therefore serves as a second line of defence
- If the seller does not tell the purchaser the truth or does not tell the purchaser the whole story in response to questions, the buyer might find that there are very few practical remedies. Oral misrepresentations are notoriously difficult to prove and so purchasers usually seek express representations

Conclusion

One of the secrets of due diligence is knowing what is required, from whom, and when. In other words, project management is key. Start right at the very beginning. Why you are doing the deal and what you hope it will achieve are vital pointers as to what areas due diligence needs to cover and to what extent. However, there are few right answers. What and how much to cover in any deal is ultimately a matter of judgement.

Managing the project means managing not just advisers – the subject of the next chapter – but managing the seller and its advisers also. Obstacles to honest investigation cannot be helped, but they can be managed.

One of the big benefits of a properly executed due diligence programme is that it highlights areas of uncertainty that can be ring-fenced by warranties, indemnities or other forms of protection. The buyer should not regard either due diligence or legal protection as substitutes for each other. They are separate, complementary weapons to be used in tandem.

3   Working with advisers

There are many advantages for buyers who choose to carry out their own due diligence. However, the pace of the deal and the diverse range of expertise needed means that advisers are usually a feature. It is very important to select the right ones and to get the best out of them.

Managing advisers means controlling the process from the beginning. This includes spending time planning and briefing them properly. As self-evident as that may sound, it is surprising how often advisers receive an inadequate initial briefing. At the very least, it should include:

- The reason for the transaction
- The structure of the transaction: shares or assets?
- The rationale for the work. For example, if its purpose is to satisfy lenders, the consultants need to know this. Lenders will typically take a much more conservative line than a purchaser
- Existing knowledge and major concerns

Advisers cannot be expected to produce what you want if you do not know yourself and/or you do not tell them what it is. They also know that it is difficult to be sued if they provide too much data. You do not want tea chests full of photocopied contracts from your legal advisers. As with all advisers, you want an evaluation and recommendations from people who are supposed to be experts in their field. And, of course, all advisers always seek to 'add value' so that they can charge more.

Selecting advisers

The most reliable way to select the right advisers is to build relationships with them. To find individual advisers who have expertise and integrity, ask people's opinions. Take time to meet them and get references from previous clients to understand exactly what their role was and how they performed.

Technical ability and experience count for a lot, but so do personal chemistry and seeing what lies behind the typical adviser's sales veneer. The key to getting on in a professional services firm is bringing in business. There are plenty of clever and experienced advisers out there. What every acquirer needs is clever and experienced advisers who are looking out for their best interests and not just interested in getting a deal done to earn a fee.

Understand also how far they are prepared to go in giving opinions. Financial advisers, for example, should be expected to give a view on at least the quality of any projections and not merely a description of them.

Experience and skills

After interpersonal factors comes the right mix of experience and skills. Experience required, in order of importance, is:

1. Experience of carrying out due diligence
2. Experience of the purchaser
3. Experience of the target company's sector

In other words, the most important skill is preparing due diligence reports for different companies; knowing the purchaser and the sector are additional benefits.

The team

Although the reputation of the firm is important, the individual qualities of the team are most important. You do not want to be lumbered with the 'B' team. In gauging this, remember that due diligence is about the right people asking the right questions of the right sources. The right people need more than just analytical skills and a good grasp of accounting standards or whatever. Analysis is important, but so is tenacity, street-wise detective work and experience and judgement. For these reasons, a buyer should make sure the team consists of appropriately experienced advisers. The key to profitability in a professional services firm is pushing as much work as possible down to the lower levels of the organisation. All too often, the senior adviser will 'sell' the work, then disappear, leaving more junior staff to complete it, only to pop up again at the final presentation.

Timetable

A typical due diligence assignment takes advisers at least three weeks. It can be shortened but if it is, there is a danger that quality will suffer. Putting more people onto it to compensate is no guarantee that the analysis will be carried out with enough thought or thoroughness.

Give advisers as much time as possible and involve them as early as possible. Even if the deal has not been finalised, it is still worth calling them in. They can begin to plan the work, think about putting a team together and even start some of the background research. Involving advisers early also allows you to pick their brains. Thinking through terms of reference with them in the early stages is time well spent. The other side of the coin is that if you involve advisers late, they charge more.

Under the heading of timetable, it pays also to consider the sequence in which due diligence advisers are deployed. The legal and financial teams are relatively expensive. It is pointless letting them get started if there are still doubts about the deal. If, for example, the deal involves a site with potential environmental liabilities, you may want to get an interim report from a firm of environmental specialists before giving the go-ahead to the other advisers.

Written terms of reference

What you expect each specialist to do, by when and for how much, should be properly reflected in writing.

The written engagement letter for each adviser sets out:

- The scope of the work
- A clear demarcation of responsibilities, possibly showing how one adviser's brief fits with other advisers' work
- To whom the adviser owes a duty of care
- Their timetable
- Whether an interim report or presentation is needed
- Fees
- Headings to be covered in the report
- Who will manage the assignment
- Confidentiality
- The rights to the results
- Assignability of the results
- Liability insurance (if appropriate)
- What happens if the deal is abandoned and the work is terminated early

Fees

Advisers will maintain that you get what you pay for and, in any case, the choice of consultant should not be overly cost driven. The reputation and experience standing behind opinions are more important than simple fee considerations. To an extent, they are right, but a firm of advisers will still charge what it thinks it can get away with. If it sees the prospective buyer as having deep pockets or as too inexperienced to know any better, the proposed fee will be higher than if it thinks it is dealing with a mean and experienced acquirer. It is worth haggling.

It is normal for due diligence to be carried out on the basis of a fixed fee. Although it is difficult to estimate how many hours a due diligence exercise will consume, it is up to advisers to get their estimates right. and therefore a buyer should be reluctant to vary fee levels unless there is a change in the scope of work or delays outside the adviser's control. In the event of either, it is up to the adviser to convince the buyer of the need for additional fees.

Contingent fees are common. Here the fee depends on whether or not the deal completes. The usual arrangement is for there to be a discount on the fee if the deal does not go ahead, and an uplift if it does. How much the fee varies around the 'normal' is really up to the adviser and the buyer to negotiate. Contingent fee arrangements can vary from a small up/down right through to 100 per cent success fees (i.e. nothing if the deal does not complete but a considerable uplift if it does). Although contingent fees are a good way to minimise costs if a deal does not go ahead, it is better to avoid fee arrangements that give advisers too much of a material interest in the transaction completing.

The fairest mechanism is one that at least allows the advisers to break even if the deal does not go ahead, but gives them a reward if it does. As a rough rule of thumb, one third of the price of a due diligence exercise will be profit. On a contingent fee basis, this would mean knocking off a third of the fee if the deal aborts and adding up to the same again onto the 'normal' price if it completes.

Liability caps

Some advisers seek to cap their liability by limiting their liability should the client prove negligence.

Liability caps are hard to justify. If the job is done properly, the adviser has nothing to worry about. At the very least, the prospective client is owed a full explanation of why advisers deem it necessary to cap their liabilities. If the buyer is not satisfied, it should say so and perhaps go elsewhere.

Plan the work

Probably the next most important contribution to successful due diligence is planning how the work will be carried out.

Much due diligence involves analysing information supplied by the target company and interviewing members of its management team. In order to ensure that time is not wasted and that the information and people are available, it is vital that planning takes place in conjunction with target company management. There is little point in teams of expensive advisers arriving at a company only to find that the key people are not available or that it will take time to provide the information that they require.

It is therefore vital that the target is supplied early on with information requests and a list of the people to be interviewed. Whilst more information and more interviews will normally be required during the course of the work, this initial planning should greatly help to ensure that the work is carried out efficiently.

Co-ordination

Someone should be responsible for running the entire due diligence programme. One person looking at the whole picture prevents potentially serious issues from falling between the cracks. Exactly who depends on company style and on the deal. In small and medium-sized companies, co-ordinating due diligence might fall to the chief executive. In larger companies, it may be the manager of the division that will run the company once acquired, the in-house lawyer or an individual with responsibility for carrying out acquisitions.

There are advantages and disadvantages to each. The business unit should bring more sector understanding. If, on the other hand, acquisition specialists do the work, they can build on the experience of previous deals. Because of the need to think about the integration plan from the start, they should involve the operators at an early stage.

If co-ordination is not done in-house, the adviser who is closest to the commercial negotiations should be appointed.

There is also a job of co-ordination to be done with various in house experts.

- What are the objectives and concerns of the line managers who either know the business or will run it afterwards?
- Internally, who are the main points of contact? Who has authority for what? What are the main areas of responsibility?
- Internal advisers (tax, property, etc.) may have excellent knowledge which can be applied to the target business. How are they to be used?
- Will the project manager act as the main interface between the internal experts, the commercial team and outside advisers, or will the outside advisers have direct access?

Communicate regularly

Whoever is co-ordinating due diligence should make sure there is regular communication with the advisers. Communication should not be a one-off event which takes place when the finished report is presented. This is not to say that there should be formal progress meetings on a weekly basis – the deal timetable is usually too short for that – but there should be reasonably regular updates from external advisers as the enquiries proceed. If nothing else, this allows the buyer to:

- Communicate changes in its concerns
- Identify significant issues early on
- Make sure all advisers' efforts are co-ordinated

Also hold regular meetings internally so that:

- The commercial impact of what is being found out can be properly assessed, questions can be raised and fed back to the investigating advisers and areas where further investigation is needed can be identified. If there are issues which kill the deal, the sooner these are brought up, the better
- The due diligence process itself can be evaluated. Are you getting what you want?

Left to their own devices, advisers will work independently of each other. Encourage them to work together. For example, lawyers will examine legal structure and may find that liabilities will be triggered if the target leaves its present group. These could, for example, be capital gains tax liabilities because of inter-group transfers of assets or additional costs because the target company can no longer benefit from group discounts. The accountants need to build these into their model.

Report

The form of report is important to managing the process.

A written report is not just a record but fulfils several functions, such as keeping all parties informed of matters arising. There is also a lot to be said for insisting on a presentation. This is the opportunity to pin advisers down as to what they really think. The opinions of experienced due diligence advisers are extremely important.

Due diligence reports should be user friendly and contain an executive summary. The executive summary is the most important part, as it is the only part many recipients will actually read. Reports can be anything from three bullets or 300 pages long. Be clear from the outset about what you want.

Post-acquisition

Acquirers need a mechanism for identifying possible warranty and indemnity claims which may come to light after completion. It is best to make someone responsible for this and to make sure that operating management understands what claims may be possible. They will need to be fully briefed on the claims procedure and time limits. The statutory limitation period for notifying warranty and indemnity claims is 6 years or 12 years from the sale. Negotiated limitation periods can be as low as 2 years. Sale and purchase agreements often contain formal notification procedures for dealing with warranty and indemnity claims.

Conclusion

A due diligence programme is likely to involve a number of different advisers. Even when the target is a business the acquirer knows well, external advice can add value to a transaction. How much value will be influenced by how well due diligence is managed. Planning, co-ordination and communication are as important as any other input.

It is an obvious point, but advisers cannot be expected to perform to their full potential if they are not properly briefed, do not understand the brief or are not kept informed of relevant findings of other advisers. If in doubt, over-communicate.

Getting the best out of advisers also means using the right ones. A mix of technical ability, chemistry, due diligence experience, possibly sector experience, fees and the degree of involvement by senior professionals all play a part in the final choice. One thing is certain: you will not have time to get to know advisers in the heat of a deal, so get to know and select them before the pressure is on. Then you can involve them at the earliest possible stage.

Finally, you need a user friendly written report, with an executive summary and a presentation that gives you the chance to probe for opinions.

4 Financial due diligence

Very few deals are carried out without financial due diligence (FDD). Accounting is not a science. All accounts are subject to judgement and contain 'one-off' profits or expenses which distort profitability. This means that even audited accounts contain many questions for a purchaser. One of the main jobs of due diligence accountants is to undo what has been done by other accountants. There is a lot more to financial due diligence than just blessing the target's financials. Good financial due diligence aims to give a view of underlying profit which can be used, if not to predict the future, then to provide a canvas on which the picture of the future can be painted. Reporting accountants can also be a good source of non-financial business information.

Aims

Until a firm offer is made, the vendor will have controlled information. Anything provided will have presented the target company in its best light. This is the acquirer's opportunity to:

- Be satisfied that the target's financials give an honest picture of its trading performance
- Make sure there are no skeletons in the cupboard big enough to break the deal, while presenting an opportunity to find as many smaller skeletons as possible for use in the final negotiations
- Determine the net debt position and any seasonality, and hence working capital requirements thought the year. Explained below, this is central to any 'cash free/debt free' clauses in the acquisition agreement
- Look at alternative ways of structuring the transaction
- Take a view on underlying profitability and thereby have a basis for forecasting future performance

- Confirm that the target fits its acquisition strategy
- Confirm the deliverability of synergy assumptions

The accountants will offer a much fuller scope, arguing that their people spend a relatively long time interviewing target management and can therefore unearth all sorts of secrets and make all sorts of judgements. While this may be true, any adviser with any respect for its client would surely bring up other, non-financial concerns it may have without being mandated to do so. Besides, the quality of their judgements relies on the people doing the work. Given that the bulk of the work, including management interviews, will be pushed down to the very lowest levels, the quality of those judgements must be questioned. However, reporting accountants can provide a valuable second opinion therefore if there are any niggling non-financial doubts by all means include specific questions in the terms of reference.

Financial due diligence is not an audit

FDD is not an audit. The aim of an audit is to verify results. Due diligence seeks to explain those results. It begins with information supplied by the company and supports this by interviewing key members of the management team and by reviewing the auditors' working papers. It takes reported results and arrives at underlying profitability after examining accounting policies and their application and isolating exceptional income and costs. It does not normally involve the independent verification of the financial information given. Inevitably, FDD relies more on 'soft' issues than an audit, involves a lot more uncertainty and calls for a great deal more judgement and, something to bear in mind if the Finance Director insists on using your auditors to carry out FDD, may call for a different type of accountant.

The financial due diligence team will try to speak to the auditors and review the audit files for the last two to three years and, if they are also looking at tax, the tax files for up to the last six. They will do this at an early stage to try to get a picture of how thoroughly the numbers have been scrutinised. In return, the auditors will want an indemnity against any legal action which may come as a result of allowing access to their working papers and confirmation from the investigating accountants that nothing can be relied upon and that everything will be kept confidential. As there is little incentive for the auditors to co-operate and every risk if they do, an investigating accountant who wants to see their papers has little choice but to accept.

Terms of reference

The reason why financial due diligence reports are often long and boring is that the accountants have not been told what is of real importance. FDD is carried out by people who trained as auditors. An audit is very prescriptive. In contrast, there is very little guidance from the profession on non-audit investigations. They need to be told what to do – in particular, what must be confirmed and what must not be true for the deal to go ahead.

Another key is for the reporting accountants, as with all due diligence advisers, to understand the context in which their report is being prepared. For example, if the acquisition rationale is to gain market share but fold all operations into the acquirer's existing facilities, the investigation will have a different focus than if it is to enter a new product market and keep the acquired operation running.

Demarcation is also called for. Some of the areas with which FDD could get involved – tax and pensions, for example – could also be covered by other advisers. Make sure it is clear to everyone who is doing what (while banging the table on the importance of advisers working together). All too often, advisers duplicate each other's work or try to improve on the efforts of others if their respective roles are not properly defined.

Cross-border considerations

Local advice is key. Financial statements may look very similar, but despite various directives on company accounts and more of a willingness to adopt international standards, there remain considerable differences between the accounting policies employed around the world, and considerable philosophical differences, too. In many countries, taxation is the dominant influence on the accounts. This means that, for example, deprecation rates may reflect more what the tax authorities want than what is economically appropriate for the business.

Because of the lack of effective harmonisation, the analysis of financials can be a long and drawn out affair if the target has operations in a number of different countries. This will need to be factored into the timetable.

The work

The first port of call for the investigating accountants will rarely be the finance team. First, they should speak to those who are responsible for the company's commercial operations to gain an understanding of the company's history, strategy, competitive environment, purchasing and sales, marketing and production operations. A proper understanding of the business leads to a much more meaningful interpretation of its financial results.

The accountants start with the historical results. These provide an objective benchmark on which to base a valuation and estimate future earnings. It is important to obtain comfort that past performance is honestly presented and that it is indicative of the future, to strip past results of non-recurring and/or unusual items, to adjust costs (especially compensation costs in owner managed and privately held businesses) to reflect the market value for services rendered and to exclude income or expenses derived from redundant assets (these will be valued separately from the continuing operations).

Trading performance

This section analyses the historical profit and loss account for the business for the last 3 to 6 years, together with the most recent management accounts. The approach is to take each category of income and expense and do the following:

- Break down summary figures so that their composition can be understood. Thus FDD will show, for example:
  - Sales and gross profit by activity and geography
  - The components of, for example, sales and marketing costs, on year by year basis
- Analyse the trend in results to understand:
  - Any unusual items
  - The relationship between the figures
- Identify any underlying patterns
- Show where the profits come from. Which products are most profitable? Have profits come from trading or, at the other extreme, from a one-off insurance claim?
- Are there any obvious vulnerabilities, such as dependencies on major customers or major contracts?
- Look at performance versus budget for the year to date and its impact on the full year forecast
- Analyse seasonality
- Reconcile profit and cash flow. There are often good reasons why they differ, and often there are not

Analysing the trend in results

Getting behind the numbers is where financial due diligence provides the real value. Where acquisition price is based on a multiple of profit, the biggest wins come not from isolating non-recurring items, but from unearthing a profit figure which is higher than it should be. Changing accounting policies is one way to massage profit, but most investigating accountants should be alive to that sort of manipulation. More subtle are the 'judgements' which go into constructing a profit and loss account. Imprudent revenue recognition or the deferral of costs by including them in the balance sheet are the most frequent means of pushing up reported profitability. Generally speaking, these will lead to differences between profit and cash flow. Sadly, cash flow is often neglected when analysing financial statements. Any serious discrepancies between profit and cash should arouse suspicion and be explained. Gross margin is another figure to analyse very carefully, and an explanation for any changes needs to be pursued until there is a satisfactory explanation.

Table 4.1 shows the areas of risk to the profit and loss account which FDD should watch out for:

Table 4.1 P&L manipulations and other traps for the unwary

Pre-deal P&L issue	*Post-deal consequences*
• Sales have been temporarily inflated or brought forward by 'channel stuffing'. • Management have resorted to inappropriate revenue recognition in seeking to drive the numbers rather than the business. • Generally, sales are dependent on sales effort rather than long-term contracts or commitments. • Attempts to increase sales pre-deal have failed.	• A significant increase in the number of credit notes • Sales drop off rapidly, e.g. because major customers do not re-order or do not re-order for some time • There is a need to reverse sales (and profits) booked (especially applicable to work carried out on contracts which span more than one accounting year) • If management have taken their eye off the ball during the sale process, post-deal sales may fall off because of a lack of pre-deal sales effort. • Increased advertising, for example, has failed to stimulate sales. Potential of the business is less than originally thought.
• Sales and cost of sales not matched.	• This is more common in some industries than others. Where actual payments and/or costs are spread over a long period, it is clearly much easier than with a cash business to recognise sales ahead of costs. Similarly, it is quite common, for example, in the construction industry to find large and complex projects spread over more than one financial year and, with many of them, a chance that there will be claims some years after completion. Again, the scope for taking profits early by mis-matching sales and costs is high.

(Continued)

Table 4.1 (Continued)

Pre-deal P&L issue	Post-deal consequences
• Costs are unsustainably low because current depreciation policies are inappropriate for the future.	• In some industries, for example computer software, assets lose their value quickly and need replacing on a regular basis. If assets have been fully written off, recent depreciation will have been low. However, if those assets need replacing in the near future, depreciation will soon be back to much higher levels and profits will suffer accordingly.
• Costs deferred by carrying them forward in closing stock.	• See under stock below.
• Costs deferred/reduced by being capitalised.	• Interest on borrowings used to finance the construction of fixed assets. • R&D capitalised. Not only is the charge to profits reduced, but also deferred as the capitalised costs do not need to be amortised until the programme comes into commercial production.
• Material costs dependent on a few suppliers.	• The buyer should be concerned about special pre-sale deals and the possibility that suppliers will take advantage of a change in ownership to increase prices.
• Labour costs kept artificially low.	• Pre-sales promises made about pay increases or bonuses which the buyer will have to honour • Cash payments made to avoid national insurance costs • No accruals made for holiday pay/bonuses
• Cost of sales kept artificially low.	• Inter-group transfer prices or related party transactions could be used to keep target cost of sales below normal. • 'Normal' quantity discounts over-estimated and over accrued.
• Looming liabilities not provided for.	• The basic rule which runs through accounting is that losses should be recognised and provided for as soon as they are discovered, while profits should only be accounted for when they are realised. It is a rule which is often broken. The uncertainty around losses crystallising allows them to be fairly easily dismissed, especially when crystallisation may be some way off.

Accounting judgements are one thing, but there are other means by which short-term profits can be manipulated, especially if a target has spent the last few years grooming itself for sale. It is possible, for example, to increase short- or medium-term profits at the expense of the long-term health of the business. Financial due diligence should seek to identify any such manipulations. The most common is cutting back on investments that would normally be charged to the P&L, such as research, development, marketing and training. The consequences of short-term profit improvement also need to be understood. Cutting the cost of a branded product by using lower quality raw materials or switching production to low cost countries may cause a loss of confidence in the brand. This is where commercial due diligence takes over from financial and provides yet another example of why advisers must be made to work together. The financial team can identify profit improvements which are possibly detrimental to the long-term health of the target business, and the commercial team can assess their consequences.

Accounting policies and practices

Different accounting policies could mean two identical businesses reporting very different results. Different interpretation of those policies can play a major part, too. The FDD team must report on changes in policy, but – easier said than done – also be looking out for changes in the application of those policies. Consistency and comparability may be even more difficult in cross-border transactions, where differences of definition can also play their part in clouding the numbers. Typically, an FDD team will report on the following:

- A summary of accounting policies and treatments
- Whether the accounting policies and treatments comply with generally accepted accounting standards
- An explanation of any that are unacceptable
- Whether, and to what extent, accounting policies and treatments are consistent with the policies adopted by the purchaser
- Whether accounting policies and treatments been applied consistently during the period under review

Information systems and accounting

The quality of the information system is fundamental to the whole financial due diligence exercise because of the impact on the reliability of financial information. The target's ability to produce timely and accurate monthly management accounts is one indicator of how well managed the target is. FDD is generally concerned with the following.

Management information

The accountants should have seen enough management information systems to be able to give an opinion on the quality of the target's. This is what to expect:

- An overview of management information systems
- A description of the main management information reports produced by the company
- A review and assessment of the costing systems
- Management's assessment of whether they have sufficiently accurate and timely information to allow them to monitor and control the business and to react to any opportunities or threats
- Management's views on the future development of systems
- Reporting accountants' opinion on the effectiveness of the information systems
- A summary of weaknesses which need to be addressed

Control procedures

Here again, the accountants should be able to give a reliable opinion on the quality of the systems for managing and controlling the main financial functions of the company, e.g.:

- The effectiveness of the budgetary and forecasting processes
- How well credit control and debtor collection operates
- Whether the books and control accounts (debtors, creditors, bank account and cash) are regularly balanced and reconciled

Computer systems may be covered by IT specialists, but if not, reporting accountants will normally describe the main computer systems, review third party maintenance contracts, report on software ownership and maintenance, security and back up arrangements and assess the adequacy of the systems for present and future needs

Balance sheets

The approach to the balance sheet is similar to that for the profit and loss analysis. Each significant asset and liability is examined to ensure that:

- The basis of valuation appears reasonable
- There has been no distortion in the trend

- Assets and liabilities are properly recorded. (It is not unknown for crucial assets not to be owned by the business or for liabilities not to have crystallised . . . yet)

Some of the issues which might be considered under each of the balance sheet headings are covered in the following sections.

Fixed assets

The aim is to assess whether the fixed assets are consistently and reasonably valued and whether they are adequate to support the projected future earnings of the company:

- Are intangible assets reasonably valued?
- What is the composition of fixed assets, and how have their values been arrived at?
- Are there detailed registers and analyses?
- Have there been any recent independent valuations?
- Are the depreciation policies reasonable and consistently applied?
- Does the company have clear title to its main assets?
- Has the company capitalised interest or own labour within fixed assets?
- What capital commitments are there?
- What capital expenditure is required?

The crunch is the second half of the sentence above: 'are [the fixed assets] adequate to support the projected future earnings of the company?' When grooming a company for sale, reducing investment is a good way of flattering both profits (by reducing depreciation) and cash flow. Trawling through the investment numbers over several years may reveal a falloff in investment, but just as effective are the accountants' interviews with those on the receiving end of restricted investment – production, operational and technical management.

Stock and work in progress

Stock is the only item which appears in both the profit and loss account and the balance sheet. Given the amount of discretion used in stock valuations, the scope for short-term profit manipulation and the number of times significant mis-statements of accounts turn out to be due to inflated or deflated stock, this is one of the most critical areas for investigation. Relatively small errors in the valuation of stock and work in progress can significantly distort the overall trend in the results of the company.

The key is to ensure that the approach to stock and work in progress is acceptable and has been consistent throughout the period under review. This means looking at the basis of valuation, particularly where overheads are included, and at how slow moving or obsolete stock is identified and provided for. The importance of 'seeing things through' in due diligence is particularly important here. For example, it would be wise to pin down the extent to which movements in gross margin have been influenced by stock values.

Debtors and receivables

Debtors and receivables is another area for careful investigation. Again, it is important to establish whether the approach has been consistent and whether the making and release of provisions, or the writing off or writing back of a bad debt, could have distorted the trend in the results.

The recoverability of the debtors in the most recent balance sheet will be important:

- Is the debtor age profile acceptable?
- What is the trend?
- Is there an acceptable system for establishing and enforcing credit terms?
- Are bad debt reserves created on a reasonable (and consistent) basis?
- What is the past experience with bad debts?
- Is the business vulnerable to large debtors defaulting?

Creditors and other liabilities

These should be analysed in order to identify any liabilities which have not been disclosed or any unusual items or trends in relation to the company's creditors:

- Does the company receive any special credit terms?
- Is the business under creditor pressure?
- Are there any long-term liabilities, such as hire purchase and finance lease obligations?
- Are there any loans from shareholders that could be repayable in the short term?
- Are the liabilities reported in the balance sheet reasonable? Every business has liabilities which are not recorded and every long-term or contingent liability that is recorded is subjective. For example, are warranty provisions in line with what might be expected from warranty terms and product performance?

However long or thorough the investigation, no accountant can be sure of finding every relevant unrecorded liability. The more experienced will get pretty close because they will know how to look. They will make a point of reading Board Minutes or the minutes of other management meetings for signs of trouble. Managers are usually quick to report anything that may cause them trouble, and they will rely heavily on their interviews with non-financial as well as financial managers.

Cash free/debt free

The price of a business is usually negotiated free of debt and cash. The parties first agree on a price for the business, excluding cash and debts, but including adequate working capital. A set of accounts is drawn up at completion and the price adjusted by adding an amount corresponding to the target company's cash and cash equivalents, deducting the target company's debt and adjusting for any differences between actual and adequate working capital.

In theory, this works because the bid price is fixed and is not affected by changes in the business between signing and closing. Problems arise because there are no generally accepted definitions of cash, debt or working capital. For example, debt can also include debt-like items such as pension provisions, lease liabilities and customer advances. These have to be negotiated.

As Table 4.2 shows, the gap between the headline price and the price paid can be significant:

Financial due diligence should provide an insight into the seasonality of the business, a 'normal' level of working capital for the cash free/debt free calculation and an input into the definitions of cash and debt.

Share capital and reserves

Details of the share capital, together with any options or rights attaching to the shares, will have to be covered, along with an explanation of any changes to the share capital and reserves during the period under review, and whether there are any unusual reserves or restrictions on distributions to shareholders. Much of the factual information here overlaps with legal. Let the lawyers report on the facts. The value the accountants can add from their management interviews is to paint a picture of how the target really works. Changes in management and shareholdings can happen for perfectly understandable reasons. They can also happen because the majority shareholder is a psychopath. If, for example, the intention is to integrate the business

Table 4.2 Headline price to price paid

£000			Notes
Bankers/IM enterprise value		**1,234**	Initial valuation
Due diligence/current performance adjustments		(133)	
Pension shortfall		(16)	
Capex underspend		(5)	
Agreed enterprise value (cash free/ debt free price)		**1,080**	Headline "price" in SPA
Plus £x for cash inherited	220		
Less £x for debt inherited	(334)		
Net debt adjustment		**(114)**	
Plus £x for actual working capital	454		
Less normal working capital	(580)		
Working capital adjustment		**(126)**	
Purchase price (equity value)		**840**	Cash actually paid to seller

with yours with him running the combined operation, you should know how he operates. The accountants should be encouraged to give a view.

Cash flow

Cash flow is as widely used in valuation as profit. FDD must report on the relationship between profit and cash generation. Ideally, the two should be the same, but they rarely are. There can be very good reasons for this. On the other hand, it could be down to poor cash management which, for example, could manifest itself as frequent breaches of overdraft limits.

Taxation

Lawyers, accountants or tax specialists may carry out tax due diligence. The aim is to assess whether the target's tax provisions are adequate and whether there is a risk of additional tax liabilities emerging (see Chapter 10). Whoever does it must liaise closely with the financial and legal advisers to ensure that information is properly shared, that nothing falls between the cracks and that there is no duplication of effort. Even if they are not doing the tax, the investigating accountants can be good information gatherers for the tax specialists. This leaves them with the role of commenting on how up to date the target's tax affairs are and whether there are disputes, taxes overdue or investigations pending. They should also give an assessment on how aggressive the target company has been with its tax planning.

Prospects

In many acquisitions, this is the nub of the whole exercise, and you certainly want the accountants' view on what the future holds. The accountants, on the other hand, will want to confine themselves to a review of the target's forecasts. Typically, they will set out to answer the following questions:

- Have the forecasts been correctly compiled on the basis of the stated assumptions?
- Are those assumptions reasonable?
- Are they clerically accurate?
- Are the accounting policies used consistent with the usual policies?
- How accurate has forecasting been in the past?
- Are the forecasts consistent with the trends in the management accounts?
- What are the vulnerabilities?
- What are the key sensitivities in the forecast?

The typical forecast for any business is a 'hockey stick' a couple of years out. Accountants should always seek to separate the reasons why the future is going to be so much better (for example, new products and new customers in the pipeline) from management's wishful thinking.

No forecast is ever right. Due diligence is more about understanding the range of possible outcomes and the risks inherent in the business. Press for opinions on likely outcomes and on the believability of management's assumptions on top of the usual mechanical application of what-ifs.

Other issues

Financial due diligence might also cover:

- Markets and competitors – with as much emphasis on analysis, market dynamics and market drivers as on fact-finding
- Sales and marketing – the aim being to probe for vulnerabilities. Credit notes, unpaid bills, invoice disputes and warranty claims could all be evidence of something fundamentally wrong with the business and its inability to maintain market share
- Purchasing and supplies. Underlying profit could be severely affected by unstable prices, a dependency on a few suppliers, frequent disruptions and no alternative supply sources
- Production – with a focus on the future. Are there any constraints on capacity? Is a costly overhaul going to be needed in the near future? How well do production facilities compare with those of the competition?

Are lead times under control and on a par with industry standards? Do research and production work effectively together?

- Premises – adequacy to meet growth plans, recent valuations, dilapidations
- Human resources. This is not just about collecting facts, explaining and commenting on organisation structure, reporting lines and so on. For a start, the accountants should have a view on management, having spent a number of weeks in their close proximity. They should also be able to take a view on the impact of other human resources issues for future profitability.

Conclusion

You will not feel comfortable if you do not commission financial due diligence. The challenge is to get good value. The term 'Reporting Accountants' is a good one because, left to their own devices, they will only report. This is not all bad. You need to understand the 'routine' accounting issues, you need to understand underlying profit, you need an assurance that the balance sheet is clean and that the profit and loss account has not been overly manipulated. If you employ accountants to cover pensions and tax, you will certainly want them to make sure that there is nothing which is going to come back to bite you. But you should want more. You want firm opinions from the accountants on the quality of the target – on non-financial as well as financial matters. More than any other adviser, these are the people who will spend most time closely observing the target and its management.

5　Legal due diligence

Legal due diligence is central to the entire due diligence programme because it forms the basis for the sale and purchase agreement. It is undertaken to achieve three objectives:

- To quantify liabilities – both recorded and unrecorded
- To find any legal or contractual obstacles
- To form the basis of the final agreement

In addition to what is set out below, lawyers could end up covering many of the topics covered in subsequent chapters. Their output should be as commercial as it is legal. Lawyers are trained to spot problems, but allowing them merely to point out problems is not enough. What a buyer needs is for the legal advisers to focus on the commercial implications of their findings.

Uncovering potential liabilities

In an asset sale, the purchaser does not normally take over liabilities unless it specifically contracts with the seller to take them over (employment liabilities being an exception). If a company is being bought, on the other hand, it comes with all its liabilities.

Liabilities come in three guises:

- Actual
- Future
- Contingent

The target will have quantified, recorded and maybe even provided for some liabilities but not others. As well as verifying the size of known liabilities, the purchaser of a company should make as certain as is possible that there are no sizeable unrecognised liabilities.

Contracts could be a source of unforeseen liabilities. Lawyers will review major contracts and agreements, first to make sure they contain no nasties and second to make sure they can be transferred to the purchaser. While change of control clauses are useful for certainty and stability, they also present an opportunity to renegotiate. As well as commercial contracts, there will be financial obligations that the investigation should also cover such as loan agreements, charges, guarantees and indemnities.

Another source of potential liabilities is litigation. One of the main tasks of legal due diligence is reporting on any litigation or potential litigation. A buyer does not want a list but the lawyers' assessment of the likely damage. One element of this is gauging the chances of success or failure and likely cost. The other is spotting danger signs. A few claims for industrial deafness are neither here nor there. The same number of claims for lung damage allegedly caused by exposure to asbestos is another matter.

The lawyers will also look closely at legal structure. Legal structure is important because there can be problems when a company leaves a group. An obvious problem is a capital gains liability being triggered because of inter-group transfers of assets. Less obvious is a target company no longer being able to benefit from group discounts.

Legal and contractual obstacles

Title

Buying a company means buying its shares. The lawyers need to check that the people selling the shares actually own them and that they have no liabilities attached which will become the responsibility of the buyer. This means:

- Inspecting documents relating to the allotment, issue, registration and transfer of shares
- Checking that former shareholders have returned their certificates and that current shareholders, or at least those who are selling their shares, have certificates
- Verifying that the shares to be sold are not subject to any charges or other encumbrances

In a similar vein, the legal investigators need to verify that the target does actually own its most important assets and that there are no charges or other encumbrances attached to them.

The purchaser will also be interested in learning about any breaches of covenant and breaches of the lease(s).

The right to domain names also needs checking. Just because a company owns a trademark does not give it the right to own the domain name.

A buyer should check that the target has the right to domain names that could be useful in the future.

Consents and releases

The sale of a company or business is likely to require a number of consents or releases. For example, a target company's shares may need release from a parent company debenture; one group of shareholders might have pre-emption rights; the deal might need merger control clearance; or there might be a need to consult with the target's Works Councils or Joint Venture Partners. The legal due diligence advisers should help identify what needs to be done so that consents and releases do not delay the transaction.

Regulatory

Lawyers need to review any licences, permissions and registrations which are necessary for lawful conduct of the target company's business. For example, in the UK a financial services business needs authorisation from the Financial Services Authority.

If the target company does require a licence to carry on business, then they should verify that this is in force and not about to be taken away. At the same time, they should check whether the acquisition would affect the licence. This should not be an issue when buying the company that holds the licences, but could be with an asset purchase or where the licences are held by another entity such as the parent company. Dealing with licencing authorities can be slow. If the lawyers cannot get comfort on licences in time, completion might have to be conditional on a licence being granted.

Special accreditations may be central to a target company's profitability. For example, it may be accredited as being able to test safety critical equipment to relevant health and safety standards. This should be checked, as standards have a habit of changing.

Local advice

Chapter 3 discusses the choice of advisers. There is one further consideration when it comes to choosing legal advisers, and that is that different due diligence topics could be governed by different laws. For example, the law under which the target company is incorporated will govern the constitution of the target and the rules about the ownership and transfer of its shares; its interests in land or property will be governed by the laws of the country in which that land or property is situated; and employment issues are likely to be governed by the laws of the countries in which the employees are based.

It is also worth remembering that in some countries the law is not the law, but a goal. Be realistic about what local legal advice can sometimes achieve.

The process

Data rooms apart, the normal starting point is for the purchaser to kick off a number of searches and at the same time to send the seller's lawyers an information request. As already mentioned, getting the questions right is a must. Sellers react badly to receiving a long list of irrelevant questions. Those questions should be framed in sufficiently broad terms to elicit all the information required.

Most of the information will come from the seller. The seller's lawyers will normally co-ordinate the preparation of responses to the questionnaire and the collection and distribution of any documentation requested.

The buyer needs to be sure that someone on his or her side keeps a careful record of what is received, when and to whom it has been circulated. There are a number of software packages around to assist with this tedious but necessary task.

It is normal for information and documentation received in response to an information request to be reviewed in a fairly mechanical way. This has a number of advantages, not least that it is a cost effective way of getting through large amounts of detailed information in a relatively short time. It should also leave the experienced practitioners more time for supervision and further investigation of the most important items. Giving experienced professionals time for selective detective work is always a good thing.

Disclosure letter

The disclosure letter itself is a source of due diligence information. Sellers often deliver the disclosure letter at the last minute, so denying a buyer the opportunity to go through it properly. Their logic is that the less time there is to comb through the information, the lower the odds of the odd controversial (and no doubt potentially expensive) item being noticed.

The purchaser should always insist that the seller delivers an early draft. The final version of the disclosure letter will not be submitted first. Disclosure letters go through numerous drafts, each disclosing more information, not least because the purchaser and its advisers should be probing and seeking further and better particulars. The process of information requesting and reviewing goes on until the purchaser is satisfied, everyone gets fed up, or the one of the principals presses the button for completion.

Other advisers

More often than not, other advisers will complete their due diligence before the legal due diligence is finished and should be encouraged to highlight any concerns which may need the legal advisers' special attention. Similarly, the legal advisers should make a point of speaking to the other advisers to make sure nothing falls between the cracks.

Public information – general background information

While the legal advisers are waiting for a reply to the information request or the first draft of the disclosure letter, they will probably build up a profile of the target from published information.

Databases

The internet and subscription databases are the first stop, although as part of the initial briefing the purchaser should have given the legal team enough general company and industry background to short circuit this stage. The investigating lawyers need to start with a good idea of the nature of the target company, its business and its affairs over the past 3–5 years to use as a guide as to where to concentrate their efforts.

Credit reference agencies

Credit reference agencies provide a credit risk assessment of the target company and give hints as to how it is regarded by the wider business community.

Companies registration office

The Register of Disqualified Directors at Companies House shows if a person has been disqualified as a director. The Land Charges Registry will reveal whether any individual seller or director has any bankruptcy proceedings outstanding or pending.

Public information – specific information

As well as using public information as a means of building up a general profile, there is an awful lot which can be used for more specific enquiries.

Property

In the UK, if property is registered, a search of the Land Registry will reveal the owner, the benefits attaching to the land and any encumbrances such as mortgages and restrictive covenants. It will also have a plan showing the boundaries of the property.

If the property is unregistered, its ownership can only be confirmed by inspecting the title deeds. However, a search at the Land Registry will reveal that it is unregistered and a search at the Land Charges Department in Plymouth will show details of mortgages, restrictive covenants, adverse easements, matrimonial land charges, etc. In the case of Limited Liability companies, Companies House information will also give details of charges against property, registered or unregistered.

In the UK, Local Authority searches will show planned changes to the area. The local land charges registry will say whether a building is listed or in a conservation area, or whether it has to comply with local planning enforcement notices.

It is not unusual for modern premises to be built on reclaimed land. There are specialist registries which show where things like coalmines and rubbish tips once were. A brand new building on a brand new office park could be a considerable burden if built on an old rubbish tip which is still giving off large quantities of methane.

Companies registration office

In some countries, there is a system for filing company documents. Companies House in the UK is a central registry which contains the target company's latest filed accounts and details of its constitution, shareholders, officers, changes in the directors and secretary and notices of appointments of receivers and liquidators, etc. There is usually a short delay in documents getting into the files, so changes made in the previous 21 days will not be on record.

As well as conducting a search on the target and its subsidiaries, the legal advisers will probably search the seller, too, just to check it has the powers to sell the target company.

Courts

Where the buyer wishes to verify the status of any pending litigation disclosed by the target, or where searches need to be made to ensure that no steps have been taken to put it into receivership or administration or to wind it up altogether, court searches can be made.

Restrictive trade practices register

In the UK, details of any registered agreement under the Fair Trading Act have to be registered. There may be restrictions registered which benefit, or which may bind, the target.

Specialists

There may be a need to bring in specialists to cover one or more of the legal due diligence areas. If specialists do need to be commissioned, extra time might be needed. Some may also need a lot more access than the seller may have initially contemplated.

Similarly, more time will be needed if there are subsidiaries or significant assets overseas requiring local lawyers to carry out some of the due diligence. Language barriers and time differences will do little to speed up the process, and cultural differences, including fundamental misunderstandings of what due diligence is about, can stop a transaction dead.

The report

Lawyers, more than anyone else, know they are not going to be sued for reporting too much. Without a proper briefing from the buyer, the legal report can be a long, incoherent, detailed, rambling affair supported by a mountain of copies of the documentation supplied by the seller.

The challenge is to manage the lawyers properly. Insist on:

- Drafts of the report
- A commentary on issues as they turn up
- An executive summary at the start of the report which identifies the major issues and gives an opinion on how they should be addressed in the sale and purchase agreement
- A presentation of findings, again covering the highlights and how to deal with them. You are paying for opinions, not words on paper

And make sure the term 'major' or 'highlights' is properly understood.

Conclusion

Legal due diligence is key to the final agreement. It covers a multitude of specialities as well as the more obvious legal areas such as title, consents and releases and regulatory issues. In addition to their own work, the lawyers must liaise closely with other due diligence providers, because what they find could be an important for the final agreement. They should communicate throughout the transaction, and their report should contain an executive summary which highlights the key *commercial* issues, with recommendations on what to do about them. A presentation of their findings allows the buyer to ask questions and to push for opinions.

6   Commercial due diligence

A company is acquired for its future profits. Commercial due diligence (CDD) is all about assessing a target's future performance by looking at its market prospects and competitive position.

CDD can also provide something more strategic. It can be structured so as to give comfort that the deal will actually work by assessing the likely strategic position of the entity post-acquisition and its ability to achieve sales growth through price increases, sales increases or both.

Where other forms of due diligence analyse company records and interview the target's management and advisers, commercial due diligence gets its information from the outside by interviewing customers, competitors and anyone else with up to date, in-depth knowledge of the market and what is going on within it. This makes commercial due diligence a complementary activity to other types of due diligence.

Scope

How much CDD to do and where to concentrate is, as ever in due diligence, a judgement based on the balance of risk and knowledge (see Figure 6.1). Factors to consider would include:

- Existing knowledge. Companies which are already active in a market should know their market. All too often, though, when companies think they know about markets they do not, or rather their knowledge is at the wrong level to assess prospects. Also, while there might be overlap between two companies, there are likely to be activities, market segments or geographical markets about which the buyer knows next to nothing
- The perceived level of risk. Buying a small company, in a familiar market, where the consequences of the deal going wrong are small and there are no unanswered integration questions, the risk is relatively low
- The need for 'political' justification or to convince investors, lenders or a sceptical board

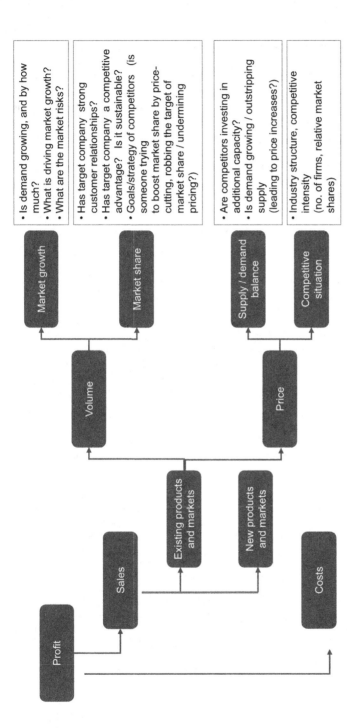

Figure 6.1 The key to CDD is disaggregating the sales figure, analysing each component and turning market data into financials

- What claims the seller has made that sound peculiar or are critical to valuation and/or the target's future – those blockbuster new products that are on the point of launch and which are going to transform the target's fortunes and reverse the long-term trend of ever deepening losses
- The reasons for the deal. If we go back to the chart in Chapter 2, as is shown in Table 6.1, the focus of CDD might be different according to the reasons for the deal

CDD can be highly tailored and, as well as the general headings of market and competitive position, could include some very specific commercial topics, such as validating the order pipeline or verifying cross-selling opportunities

Table 6.1 The commercial due diligence focus will vary with the type of deal

M&A type	Strategic objectives	CDD focus
• The overcapacity M&A	• Eliminate overcapacity, gain market share, achieve scale economies.	• Ability to retain market share, market growth, competitor reaction, relative strategic advantage post-deal.
• The geographic roll-up M&A	• A successful company expands geographically, operating units remain local.	• Strength of local operations and local management, target's ability to continue meeting customers' key purchase criteria, market growth.
• Product or market extension M&A	• Acquisitions to extend a company's product line or its international coverage.	• Strength of product relative to competition, strength of customer relationships, target's ability to continue meeting customers' key purchase criteria, market growth, competitor reaction, cross-selling opportunities, distribution/ marketing synergies.
• The M&A as R&D	• Acquisitions used instead of in-house R&D to build a market position quickly.	• Target's relative market position, industry and technological trends, customer acceptance of the product/technology, target management ability, originality of the technology being acquired, assessment of competing technologies.
• The industry convergence M&A	• A company bets that a new industry is emerging and tries to establish a position by culling resources from existing industries whose boundaries are eroding.	• Industry and technological trends, target's product/technical capability.

Overlap with financial due diligence

As financial due diligence will provide much of the information and analysis needed to form a view on commercial prospects, why go to the trouble and expense of conducting commercial due diligence? The reason is that financial due diligence collects its market and competitive information from management, whereas CDD talks to a wide a range of relevant people operating in the market. FDD and CDD should be seen as complementary. This complementarity should be recognised by ensuring the two teams work together. In addition, financial and commercial due diligence teams have access to sources and to information which can be valuable to the other. The financial due diligence will have access to debtors lists, for example. These will contain the identities of ex-customers. For obvious reasons, the CDD team likes to talk to ex-customers. In exchange, the commercial due diligence team can find and provide a wider range of estimates of market size and future growth rates, which the financial due diligence team can use to assess forecasts and scenarios.

Timing

Commercial due diligence does not have to be carried out after Heads of Terms have been negotiated, although it is much quicker and easier with target management's blessing and official access to customers and other contacts. However, there may be advantages to carrying out CDD early:

- CDD can confirm or otherwise the buyer's acquisition strategy
- CDD is the least expensive type of investigation and can provide a clear pre-acquisition stop-go decision before more expensive investigations are started
- As CDD can be conducted without the knowledge of the target it:
  - Can avoid raising the seller's expectations
  - Avoids any embarrassment if the acquisition is not progressed
  - Allows enquiries to be made without the restraints which can be imposed by Heads of Terms

Choosing the team

Commercial due diligence could be carried out by a bewildering array of providers, each of which have their own strengths and weaknesses. The main options are:

- The buyer itself
- The transaction services arms of the big accountancy firms

- A strategy consultancy
- A market research firm
- An industry expert
- Commercial due diligence specialists

Carrying out any form of due diligence in-house develops expertise and taps into internal expertise. The major constraint is the ability to deploy sufficient resources of the right calibre at the right time.

Commercial due diligence is an adjunct to the activities of due diligence accountants. It is only natural that they should offer CDD as one of their transaction services. They argue that the financial and commercial due diligence teams work together more effectively if they are from the same firm.

Some of the big strategy firms started in CDD and some still carry out commercial due diligence work on the bigger deals. Like the audit-based firms, the strategy firms have strength in both breadth and depth. They also bring great rigour to their work, which is something often missing from CDD.

Market research firms collect large amounts of data but may not synthesise it into an answer as well as some of the others. The Market Research Society in the UK actually forbids members contacting competitors, arguing that it is unethical. If a buyer knows what questions to ask and has the resources to assimilate a lot of data quickly, using market researchers for the filed work is a reasonable option.

Industry experts claim their knowledge is more pertinent and detailed than that which can be developed by outsiders. They also have a shallow learning curve, lots of contacts and should know where to delve for information. The downsides are that they can lack the necessary analytical skills and suffer from the occupational hazard that is blind acceptance of an industry's conventional wisdom.

Specialists in commercial due diligence claim to give the best of both worlds by combining the research capability of the market research firms with the analytical skills of the strategy firms. There is a lot of truth in this, although on the whole they tend towards one of the two camps.

Industry experience

With commercial due diligence, probably more than anywhere else, the question of relevant industry experience crops up as a factor in the choice of supplier. Commercial due diligence is a process which can be applied to industries almost universally. What counts is the skill of the team, not its industry knowledge or industry contacts, both of which have a habit of being irrelevant and out of date anyway. A buyer should look to the commercial due diligence team to bring highly developed information gathering and analytical skills and a good dose of solid commercial experience. Even in very specialist industries, there is a lot to be said for using seasoned specialists rather than industry experts.

This last point is a theme that crops up in all areas of due diligence. It is obviously good to have first-class minds working on an acquisition, but by their very nature due diligence exercises do not yield perfect information. There is no substitute for having at least someone on the team with hard-bitten commercial experience. The contribution of experienced professionals is doubly important in CDD. Good commercial due diligence researchers are not always good at drawing all, and sometimes even the right, conclusions from the data they collect. This is where the skills of the experienced project leader come in. The leader's role is to stand back from the detail and make sure the research answers the question. Without good, analytical, commercial project leadership, commercial due diligence exercises too easily become semi-focused collections of 'interesting' market and competitor information not joined up to financial projections.

Briefing the team

The reasons for acquiring will, to a large extent, determine what questions need to be asked. If the acquisition is intended to gain market share, stabilise market prices by knocking out a troublesome competitor or acquire a new growth product, then it helps greatly if the CDD team knows this.

Market and competitive investigations can take place at a number of levels. The level of the inquiry needs to be specified right from the start. The Chairman will have a different perspective to a subsidiary MD. Be clear from the start who the audience is.

Buyers collect a lot of information and formulate many hypotheses prior to due diligence starting. It is best to share these with the CDD team. Tempting though it might be to tell CDD advisers nothing, the only good reasons for doing this are because there is a high level of internal debate and uncertainty or because of conflicting reports from the market.

Finally, be prepared for issues to change as the study progresses. Once the first layer of uncertainty has been bottomed out, there is another, then another, followed by another. New questions arise as old ones are answered. The questions set at the beginning of a CDD exercise can therefore be very different from those which need answering at the end. There is no real way around this except to stress, once again, the benefit of staying close to the CDD team as they carry out their work.

Getting the information

There are four sources of information in commercial due diligence:

- Management
- The buyer's own organisation
- Desk research (known as secondary sources)
- Primary sources

Most commercial due diligence will start with discussions with the target's management. As well as covering the market, how it works, who is in it and how they compete, how the market segments the discussions will cover customers' key purchase criteria (KPCs) and how well the target meets them relative to the competition. How confidently the target's management answer these questions (and how robust their answers subsequently prove to be) can also contribute to management assessments.

The CDD team should be encouraged to talk to relevant internal contacts at an early stage. Confidentiality is an issue, but the discussions can be dressed up as something else. Salesmen and others with day-to-day contact in the market can be invaluable sources of information and can assist greatly in framing the overall direction of the study. Furthermore, companies often recruit from their competitors, so it is entirely possible that there are former employees of an acquisition target or of one of its competitors on the payroll.

Secondary sources are published, or publicly available. There is no comprehensive list of what these might be. The internet is the usual starting point. Trade journals are worth a look, brokers' reports can be good, published market reports can give decent background information and a broad understanding of a market, its size, growth and the relative market shares of its participants. However, secondary sources are general, rarely up-to-date, rarely cover specific niches in enough detail and are often wrong.

Primary sources

The main drawbacks of secondary information, timeliness and specificity, are countered in CDD by talking directly to people operating in the target's market, especially customers. Target management will hand pick the contacts they provide. What target management never realises when picking 'friends and family' for interview is they usually have a pretty secure relationship with the target. This makes them talk much more freely than others. Nonetheless, a good CDD house will go out of its way to find additional contacts to supplement those provided by management.

Interviews

There is a huge amount of free information available for the asking. Teasing out the best from industry participants requires semi-structured and free flowing discussions, rather than highly structured questionnaire based interviews. This in turn calls for a lot of initial research, planning and, above all, skilled researchers who are confident enough to go off script when an unexpected avenue crops up.

Unfortunately, there is not one proven ideal source. The types of respondent typically spoken to (in rough order of importance, although this tends to vary with industry) are:

* Customers
* Competitors
* Industry experts
* Former employees
* Distributors
* Specifiers

Customers

Customers are the most important group of interviewees. Talking to enough articulate customers will give the researcher a pretty reliable idea of their purchase criteria and how the various competitors measure up. From this comes a pretty good first cut at the target's strengths and weaknesses, and the opportunities and threats it faces going forward. The main objective with customers is to make sure they concentrate on the big picture and not on day-to-day issues like problems with last week's deliveries.

Customers come in three varieties.

* Past
* Present
* Non-customers

And it is important to speak to a good mix of all three.

PAST CUSTOMERS

The goal with past customers is to understand the reasons why they are no longer buying from the target. This may be completely understandable, like they no longer have a need for the target's products, or it may be something much more serious, for example, being on the receiving end of appalling service, high prices and poor quality or migrating to some new technology.

PRESENT CUSTOMERS

Present customers will be able to talk in depth about how important the product or service is to them, the target's current performance, how it rates against the competition on the KPCs, whether it is improving or getting worse, whether the KPCs are changing, how well the target is keeping up and so forth. But they are customers and, as customers, they have usually not chosen to buy from the target because they think it is useless. For this reason, customer referencing alone is not good enough.

NON-CUSTOMERS

Some of these will be the objects of the target's marketing efforts. These prospective customers will give yet another perspective on how the target rates against competitors. Others will never be customers because, for example, the target operates in a different market segment from the one which supplies them. They can provide invaluable insights into how the market really works.

One important objective of discussions with customers is to get a rating of the target relative to the competition on key purchase criteria. The starting point is to get confirmation of the key purchase criteria, by segment, both now and in the future, then how well the target performs against them relative to the competition. Market share gains will come about if the target is better than the competition.

As well as helping to rank the target against its most important competitors, customers are also usually knowledgeable about overall market trends – so, for example, they can shed light on market growth, technological trends and so forth.

Competitors

Competitors will usually have pretty forthright opinions on the strengths and weaknesses of the target company. They will usually know target management well and in some cases may even be ex-employees of the target company. They will also have views and information on the market, the way it is going and what the future might hold.

Approaching competitors is always problematical. Some researchers will not do it at all. Given their proximity to the target and its markets, discussions with competitors simply have to be a feature of CDD.

Industry experts

Specialist brokers exist to provide telephone access to vetted subject matter experts. Other frequently consulted industry observers are trade journalists.

These usually have a tremendous knowledge of their industry and the players within it, which they will gladly share.

Other industry observers include trade association officials, academics and consultants. These people often follow developments in an industry closely and are familiar with many of the major players. Talking to them can provide a good introductory briefing and provide other contacts.

Former employees

Former employees are another invaluable source of information. They can be hard to find, and their responses sometimes need treating with caution, but they can be the single most valuable source of information.

Any former employees of the target in the buyer's organisation are obvious sources of information. Otherwise, industries tend to be fairly small worlds and ex-employees will usually be found working in competitors. They can normally be found by looking through the trade press.

Interviewing former employees is even more valuable where the seller has limited access to customers and other outsiders who deal with the target business. The seller rarely remembers to include them in the confidentiality agreement.

Distributors

Distributors are crucial in many industries, especially in North America. Because of the way the market is structured there, some companies have little direct contact with the end-users of their products. Like former customers, former distributors can also be an excellent source of information, as can non-distributors. The best suppliers tend to attract the best distributors, so it pays to talk to distributors who do not handle the target's products as well as those that do.

Specifiers

In some industries, specifiers are central to the buying decision. Understanding their power relative to the ultimate buyer is important. It tends to wax and wane with the business cycle and will be more pronounced with some products than with others, but the importance, for example, of architects and surveyors as specifiers of certain building products, of GPs as specifiers of pharmaceuticals and of the IT department as specifiers of computer hardware and software, should always be allowed for.

Getting access

Sometimes sellers try to restrict access to customers and management. They may even attempt to discourage the CDD team from talking to competitors.

If a seller is reluctant to co-operate with a CDD exercise or uncertain about its consequences, the following are useful arguments in its favour:

- Customer research is a normal part of the acquisition procedure
- The work will be carried out as a customer care programme. Customer care programmes have a positive PR benefit
- The researchers know what they are doing and will not upset trading relationships. It clearly helps to be able to point to a solid track record of successful projects in the past
- The research will not include customers where the relationship with the target is particularly sensitive
- Change of ownership will not be mentioned or even implied. If pressed, the researchers will say they are doing a customer care survey and know nothing about the company
- If necessary, the seller can agree to the question set

If these fail to win the seller over, it is not the end of the world. It is better to have full access, obviously, but it is not impossible to conduct CDD without it; it just takes longer and costs more.

Cost and duration

Apart from the breadth of the original scope, the main variables which affect the cost of a commercial due diligence programme are:

- The number of interviews needed
- The type of people to be contacted
- The method of contact, i.e. the way the interviews are to be held
- The degree of access
- How willing the industry is to talk

Each of these is discussed below.

How many discussions?

Like so much in due diligence, there is no right answer to this. The number will be determined by the complexity of the target, such as the number of products and number of markets, the buyer's existing knowledge, the quality of the contacts and where the perceived risks lie. In practice, about 30 interviews is usually about right for a fairly straightforward review where there is, say, one product in one geographical market. Each additional market or product would add a further 20. This is a rough guide only. With particularly obscure markets, or demanding information requirements, a lot more will be required.

The type of people to be contacted

Getting hold of, say, a marketing director of a drug company can take a lot longer than finding and holding a detailed phone conversation with a less pressured person in an industry less concerned about confidentiality.

Method of contact

While personal meetings generate more and better information than telephone discussions, CDD timescales do not permit the luxury of personal discussions. Personal meetings take up far more time than telephone calls.

Degree of access

The more access a researcher can have, the better. Suppose a stranger calls out of the blue, claiming to be a consultant researching the market. What is the typical reaction? Usually suspicion. It gets worse. The caller really wants to ask you about your biggest supplier, but cannot say so openly. Calls like this tend, at best, to be circumspect, quick and fairly superficial. The researcher typically ends up doing a lot more calls and taking a lot longer to get decent information, and this is on top of the extra time that must be taken to find the right person to talk to. Contrast that with an introduction from the target and a cover story saying that the target has commissioned the consultants to carry out a customer care survey.

How willing the industry is to talk

Some industries are incredibly open. Others, such as many parts of the IT industry, are over researched. In many automotive companies, it is company policy not to talk to researchers. It can, therefore, be difficult to find enough of the right type of respondent willing to talk.

Why do people talk?

There is absolutely no reason for anyone to talk to a due diligence researcher, but people do because they:

* Go into sales mode
* Respond to good interviewers, who are pleasant and persuasive

- Like to help
- Like talking about themselves, which is really what they are doing when asked about their jobs
- Want to clarify their own thinking. Explaining something often forces you to get your own thoughts on the subject in order
- Might get something in return. A desk research exercise combined with introductory briefings from the client and some friendly contacts enable a good consultant to make some observations which even the most experienced market participant will find valuable. Good interviews are a two-way process, not simply about sucking information from unwitting victims

Reporting

CDD draws conclusions based on information from the market. It would be a lot to expect a CDD report to come up with a perfectly informed and verified analysis of a market and a target company's position within it in the time available. Inevitably, there will be information gaps. The important thing is to make sure the trends and factors driving profitability are properly understood. It is less important to know whether the market is worth £100m or £120m than to know that there is a new technology coming along that will cut market size by 50 per cent. In addition, there must be firm, relevant, conclusions based on solid information.

Interim reports

It is a good idea to have some form of interim reporting and a series of red lights (unacceptable negative results), but it is best not to call for a full-blown written and presented interim report. Telephone updates are best, although if the due diligence programme is being managed properly, this is going to happen anyway. Commercial due diligence tends to be cumulative in its results. Forty phone calls will yield much more than double the result of twenty.

It may sound obvious, but analysis should be logical and based on facts. Ideally, a good piece of analysis will be supported by evidence and flow in a logical sequence, such that the reader comes to the same conclusions as the report before being told what those conclusions are. All too often, consultants make the mistake of thinking that charts and diagrams in themselves constitute good analysis or, worse still, have standard templates which company rules dictate must always be completed.

Conclusions

A short executive summary should contain the conclusions. The main thrust will be 'what does the future hold for this target company as a result of doing this deal?' The conclusions should also highlight any of the deal related issues which might have a bearing on negotiations. Discussions in the market place, for example, might have revealed that the marketing director is incompetent and needs to be replaced, or that customers are intending to take their business elsewhere.

Conclusion

Commercial due diligence is the process of investigating a company and its markets. Traditionally, it has been the poor relation of legal and financial due diligence. As a discipline which, in the right hands, can provide the best available forward-looking information on a business, it is indispensable to the due diligence process. It relies heavily on primary sources to get the most up to date facts on markets and market participants. Ideally, it should look beyond the immediate deal to the competitive future of the combined entity.

7 Human resources due diligence

The aims of Human Resources (HR) due diligence will sound familiar. They are to:

- Estimate the costs and avoid the risks of proceeding:
    - Identify potential deal breakers
    - Uncover significant liabilities that can be brought to the negotiating table
- Gather the information necessary to decide how best to manage the business once the deal is done

Human resources due diligence is often presented from a legal angle, with good reason, given how much HR legislation there is. Much of this can be dealt with using a due diligence checklist, but the human factors cannot. According to some studies, employee problems are the cause of up to a half of all acquisition failures.

Planning

The precise form of human resources due diligence depends on three factors:

- The reasons for the deal
- The type of business being acquired
- The form of the transaction, i.e. whether it is a share deal or an assets deal

Planning, and not just going through the checklist, is paramount.

The reasons for the deal

For example, if buying a competitor to close it down, the concern is redundancy costs and not much more. If buying a competitor to incorporate it into existing operations, it is the terms and conditions of employment in the target relative to those of the buyer, and so on.

The type of business

A manufacturing company might be unionised and subject to collective agreements. A purchaser inherits both the agreements and the industrial relations, so there are important questions to be asked about the collective agreements and management/union relations. With people businesses, the issues tend to be more about maintaining incentives and identifying and locking in key personnel.

Share deal vs. assets deal

An asset deal lets acquirers pick and choose assets and liabilities but, in Europe, owing to the Acquired Rights Directive, not people. By comparison, a share sale is often a non-event from an employment law perspective.

Collecting information

The due diligence process begins with an information request, followed by management interviews and a review of information in the public domain, such as newspaper reports and details of employment tribunal cases.

Constraints on information gathering – the Data Protection Act

Human resources due diligence involves the disclosure of employees' personal information. Personal data is regulated by the EU Data Protection Directive, and if the target has not obtained its employees' consent to the disclosure of their personal information, the seller will almost certainly be in breach. On the other hand, the confidentiality around M&A makes it unlikely that a seller will tell employees that their personal data is to be disclosed to a potential purchaser. There is no way round this, and many legal advisers admit to ignoring the law in this area. Much employee information can be anonymised, and where this is not possible, the seller can insist on conditions on its use.

Jurisdiction

There are huge national variations in labour law across Europe, and HR custom and practice varies as well. Once again, the advice with cross-border acquisitions is to engage advisers with local employment law experience in every jurisdiction where there is a sizeable number of employees.

Topic headings

As already noted, the potential purchaser is looking not just for problem areas and negotiating points, but should also have an eye out for post-deal issues. Topics to be covered fall under six headings:

*   Employee information
*   Payroll information
*   Staff structure
*   Terms and conditions
*   Industrial relations

Employee information

Deal issues

*   Is the business complying with legislation, e.g. relating to part-time and disabled employees?
*   Are there critical areas of the business in the hands of contractors? In certain cases, say where contractors own critical intellectual property, this could be a serious drawback

Integration issues

Basic employee information, dates of birth, length of service, etc., will give a profile of the workforce and allow a view on issues such as:

*   Is the business over/under staffed?
*   Possible redundancy costs
*   Basic attitudes/how readily is the workforce is likely to accept change
*   Adequacy of the workforce. How skilled is it compared with what is wanted post-deal?
*   To what extent is the business reliant upon contractors and fixed-term and casual employees? Is this a problem?
*   Who is on maternity leave or secondment, and how is their return going to be handled?

As there are few occasions more calculated to create employee uncertainty than an acquisition, it is as well to use due diligence to prepare for employee questions. Questions are usually along the same lines:

*   Will our site close?
*   Will my terms and conditions change?
*   Will the bonus system change?

- Will I be made redundant? If so, what is the package like?
- Will I have to move/change jobs?

It is not just target employees that will be craving information; the buyer's own workforce will be feeling only slightly less apprehensive and will want answers to the same questions.

Payroll information

Deal issues

- Are there any hidden liabilities? Not properly accruing for holiday pay is a classic, as are discretionary bonuses. These are not always as 'discretionary' as a purchaser might imagine
- Is anyone paid less than the statutory minimum?
- Are there any discriminatory pay structures? e.g. different pay for men and women doing the same job, or different pension arrangements or other benefits for full time and part-time workers
- Is pay reasonable? If employees need an increase to bring them up to the going rate, this ought to be factored into the deal price

Integration issues

- Are the target's and purchaser's pay, terms and conditions and perks broadly in line, or will changes have to be made on integration?
- Do bonus or incentive schemes (e.g. share options) fit?

Staff structure

Integration issues

- Who are the key people? It is worth digging, as there may be a high degree of dependence on someone who is not particularly high up or high profile
- What is the relative importance and performance of acquired employees vs. existing employees?

Terms and conditions

Deal issues

- Are there any enhanced redundancy costs or golden parachutes? How much will these cost?

- Are there any unusual terms and conditions?
- Are there any discriminatory or illegal terms and conditions, such as non-compliance with Working Time Regulations?
- Have any contractually binding promises been made about terms and conditions post transfer? If promises have been made that are not contractual, the effect on morale of dishonouring them will have to be assessed

Integration issues

- Are there any gaps or weaknesses in employment contracts? Do they need updating in the light of legislation or to address inconsistencies? For example, if an employee has a right to permanent health insurance, it is pretty difficult to justify a clause allowing the employer to dismiss an employee for long periods of sickness
- Are there any restrictive covenants in place, such as non-solicitation clauses for employees who leave? Are they adequate and will they work? Could they be changed if necessary?

Industrial relations

Deal issues

- Buying a company with strong unionisation could lead to group unionisation by the back door or, perhaps worse, two different unions vying for dominance under the new owner
- Do sickness and disability records show up any worrying trends?
- What consultative bodies are in place? Do they comply with legislation and are they sufficient for any consultation that may be required as part of the deal?
- Are there any claims against the company (past, present and future) which will transfer (they will transfer in a share purchase)? If so, the purchaser will need indemnities.

Integration issues

- Redundancy agreements vary with business. What is the standard agreed procedure in the target? For example, there may be agreed ways of selecting people and/or there may be enhanced redundancy terms
- The industrial relations history is a valuable part of piecing together a profile of the workforce. Similarly, the extent to which grievance procedures have been used is a good indication of problems in the business

- Health and safety are again part of building up the profile. Look at the accident book. What is the health and safety record like?

Health and safety is an area where legislation has pushed more responsibility onto companies. Due diligence should review the target's compliance with the legislation, and if possible, health and safety specialists should inspect the site. Injuries lead to claims and can also lead to the need for an expensive upgrading of worker protection. In some cases, inspectors have ordered critical equipment to be shut down with potentially very expensive consequences.

Cross-border issues

European works councils

In pan-European deals, there may be a requirement to consult with a European Works Council (EWC). The right to establish EWCs applies to undertakings or groups of undertakings that have at least 1,000 employees in the Member States, including at least 150 employees in total in each of two of these states.

Where the transaction is not subject to EU rules, there is an obligation to consult Works Councils. Their role is to represent and defend the interests of the employees and can only give an opinion. They cannot veto a transaction. The obligation to consult applies to both share and asset sales.

Redundancies

If there are to be redundancies following completion, the need to understand local law becomes even more pressing. Most European countries do not give employers the free hand to hire and fire that they have in the US and, to a lesser extent, in the UK, and the law is not homogenous across Europe.

Warranties and indemnities

It is important as part of due diligence to make sure that the seller has not been up to anything which will rebound on the buyer. Personal injury claims, unfair dismissals and wages arrears should be the main concerns. As an extra precaution, it is also a good idea to get something in the sale and purchase agreement saying that the seller will contribute to the costs of any pre-transfer breaches.

Warranties for human resource issues are usually negotiated to exclude single claims below a certain amount (*de minimus*). The effect may be to exclude most employment related claims. As a host of small claims could end up costing a lot in aggregate, the purchaser may want either to set a *de minimus* for aggregate claims or use indemnities instead.

Cultural issues

Culture can have a huge impact on acquisition success, but is a slippery concept probably best thought of in terms of the beliefs that guide the behaviour of people in an organisation, leading them to behave in certain ways. It is often not properly considered as part of due diligence or post-integration planning. Whether culture matters depends on the post-acquisition plans. If the acquisition is to be integrated, it helps enormously if the two cultures are similar, and if not, that the acquirer knows what to do about it.

There are two ways of trying to understand culture. The first is the informal. Just by talking to people, it is possible to gain some pretty good impressions. For example, the physical environment and the way people behave towards you and each other, gives a lot away. Particular topics to watch are:

- Attitude to risk and uncertainty
- Attitude to rules and regulations
- Speed of change
- Speed of decision making
- Focus on the big picture rather than detail, or the other way round
- Time horizons
- The importance of hierarchy, status and the maintenance of power
- Formal vs. informal systems
- The degree of openness: how much information is shared?
- Individual vs. collective responsibility

A more formal approach would be to use some of the models developed by academics such as Miles and Snow, Charles Handy and, for profiles of national business cultures, Hampden-Turner and Trompenaars.

TUPE

TUPE applies to the transfer of employees along with, say, a contract. It does not apply to share shares.

TUPE contains far-reaching rules for the protection of employees' rights on transfer. It decrees that all employees will transfer automatically to the buyer on the same terms and conditions of employment they have with the seller. Its effect is to prevent acquirers in an asset purchase picking which employees and which employment conditions they are going to take on.

Table 7.1 highlights the differences between a TUPE transfer and a share sale:

Where an undertaking is transferred from *A* to *B*, TUPE decrees the following.

* Individuals who were employed by *A* immediately before the transfer automatically become employees of *B* from the time of the transfer, on terms and conditions they previously held with *A*.
* *B* inherits all *A*'s rights and liabilities in relation to individuals transferring. In other words, the buyer inherits all the seller's wrongdoings pre-transfer
* Union relations:

  * If the entity is not merged into the purchaser's business and thereby maintains its distinct identity, collective agreements with a trade union recognised by *A* are inherited by *B*.
  * Where *A* recognises a union as far as the transferring employees are concerned, and again if the entity maintains an identity of its own after transfer, *B* must recognise the union.

Table 7.1 A share sale vs. a TUPE transfer

Share sale	TUPE transfer
• With a share sale there is no change of employer. The company is still the employer.	• With TUPE, when the seller ceases to be the employer, the buyer becomes the employer.
• No need to consult employees about the transaction.	• There is an obligation on both seller and buyer to inform and consult employee representatives about the transaction.
• No right to claim automatic unfair dismissal.	• TUPE gives employees special protection against dismissals (either by buyer or seller) which are connected with a TUPE transfer. Such dismissals are automatically unfair unless they can be shown to be for an economic, technical or organisational reason entailing changes in the workforce. This is known as an ETO.
• Change of contract terms fairly straightforward.	• Case law has made it difficult for employers to change terms and conditions of employment in connection with a TUPE transfer – even where an employee freely consents, the employee is free to argue that that change is invalid under TUPE.

- • *A* must inform recognised trade unions about the consequences of the transfer, and *B* must provide *A* with sufficient information to enable this to be done.
- • In certain circumstances, it may be necessary for *A* or *B* to consult with recognised trade unions or elected employee representatives about the transfer. This is discussed later.

- • Criminal liabilities remain with the seller. Civil liabilities transfer
- • If employees exercise their right to object to the transfer, they will usually be deemed to have resigned.
- • Dismissal of any employee (whether before or after the transfer) for any reason connected with the transfer is automatically unfair unless the reason is 'an economic, technical or organisational reason entailing changes in the workforce' (an 'ETO Reason'). The only ETO Reasons allowed tend to be genuine redundancies or because of major restructuring. A buyer will be liable for any unfair pre-transfer dismissals made by the seller
- • TUPE does not require a new employer to continue occupational pension rights in precisely the same form. However, there is a minimum level of pension contribution which must be continued, where the transferor provided a pension

Harmonisation

In practice, the buyer of a business will often wish to harmonise the terms and conditions of employment of new employees with the terms and conditions of existing employees. Under TUPE, even if transferring employees agree to changes, they may not be allowed. The key to harmonisation is finding an operational reason for changing terms and conditions which is unrelated to the original transfer. A completely new set of benefits introduced across the board for all employees might do it.

Collective consultation

There is an obligation for the seller to inform and consult either trade union representatives or employee representatives on all TUPE transfers. Representatives must be told:

- • That a relevant transfer is to take place
- • When it is to take place
- • The reasons for it
- • The legal economic and social implications of the transfer

- The measures the employer, or the buyer, is planning to take in relation to the affected employees

If there are no plans, say so. If there are plans, the employer has an obligation to consult with representatives of those transferring. Plans could include redundancies, restructuring, contract changes and changes to working practices. Consultation must be genuine, that is, undertaken with a view to reaching agreement. The seller is duty bound to consider, and respond to, any representations made. The purchaser is required to give the seller the information it needs to discharge its consultation obligations.

Consultations must take place 'long enough before the relevant transfer' to enable consultations to take place.

There is no real way around consultation. The need to preserve confidentiality is not accepted as an excuse for not consulting. 'Special circumstances' which make it impractical to consult may be allowed, but they are few and far between. In addition, the employer must demonstrate that it has done everything it could in the circumstances to comply with its consultation obligations.

Conclusion

Although human resources can be a source of considerable risk in a deal, the importance of the human factor in successful acquisitions should never be underestimated. Human resources due diligence is not always easy because of the constraints imposed upon it by data protection legislation. It is further complicated by the different rules and regulations, even in jurisdictions with the same sources of employment law. But because of its importance, it needs to be done well. It needs to be done from both a deal and a post-deal perspective, and it must cover both 'hard' and 'soft' issues. The Acquired Rights Directive is a particularly complex and uncertain piece of legislation which complicates asset deals.

8   Management due diligence

Good management can add considerable value to an acquisition. Bad management can destroy more value than almost anything. Selecting the top team early is one of the keys to acquisition success.

Many acquirers rely on their judgement and intuition. Management due diligence provides an impartial, external perspective on management.

Management appraisals

Management appraisals seek to give an objective assessment of senior managers' capability, both individually and collectively, in the context of the challenges facing the business.

Approach

The approach generally places more emphasis on structured interviews conducted by experienced assessors than on psychometric tests. Psychometric tests do have a role to play, but they are not as acceptable to senior managers – while in the right hands, a structured interview is said to be fairly reliable.

If interviews raise particular concerns, psychometric tests may be used to give a deeper insight into an individual's predispositions, attitude, leadership style, etc. They are also particularly useful in putting together management teams.

Information collection

There are five main ways in which management appraisal information is collected. These are not mutually exclusive:

1   Documentation analysis. Reviews of CVs, job evaluations and anything else written by or about the managers being examined

2   Past-orientated interviews. Fact based, structured interviews on past performance. The theory is that the past is the best predictor of the future.
3   References. These are discussions with people who have seen the manager in action. Current and former colleagues, 360-degree feedback sessions, analysts, investors, advisers, customers and suppliers are the most obvious sources. Information from the last two groups could very easily be gathered as part of the commercial due diligence
4   Work samples. Work samples are answers to hypothetical questions. Target management is asked to answer a series of 'what-if' type questions, such as 'how would you manage the integration of these two companies?' 'In such and such a role, what would be your priorities going forward?'
5   Under certain circumstances the appraisal could also include experienced practitioners watching the team in action, and so observe the quality of their interactions and of their relationships with each other

Relative effectiveness

Past-orientated interviews are the most reliable assessment method. Reference taking is useful, but only to find out about someone's track record. It may well expose known problems, although this cannot be guaranteed. References tend to be poor predictors of future performance.

To be truly useful, interviews must be properly planned and properly carried out. They are not cosy chats, but controlled situations in which one person, the interviewer, is in charge and directs proceedings. As a rough guide, this means the interviewee doing about 85 per cent of the talking. Management assessment interviews typically last about two hours.

Interview style

•   The interview style favoured by head-hunters is one-to-one interviews, in which a genuine dialogue is established and both parties put themselves forward honestly but in the best light. Real opinions are expressed, and if difficulties are encountered, both parties will talk them through in a genuine attempt to solve them.

Interview structure

Interviews have a beginning, a middle and an end. The beginning is where important first impressions are formed. Although careful interviewers try to avoid early judgements, voice, appearance and body language are all important influencers of the interviewer's attitude, and all occur on first contact.

The early stages are also where interviewer and respondent develop rapport. 'Rapport' is a difficult term to define, but is important because it is what creates the comfortable, co-operative relationship necessary for best results.

Questions

Asking effective questions is not easy. Questions can perform five functions:

1   Collection – to fill in blanks in the CV
2   Exploration – to gain an understanding as to what lies behind the words on a CV. This is perhaps the most common form of questioning in managerial assessments. Questions should be open ended, giving the respondent complete freedom to reply without suggesting what the answer should be
3   Search. Search is different from exploration, in that we are no longer just trawling to see what comes up. Instead, we are on the trail of something we know to exist, but which may not come to the surface unless we dive in and get it. Search is very important because it should point to what makes the managers tick. Questions can relate to any part of the CV, past or present:

   •   How do you handle conflict? Tell me about the worst disagreement you have experienced during your career and what came of it
   •   How do you get ideas accepted?
   •   What do you feel was your most worthwhile achievement?
   •   What problems do you find when dealing with subordinates? How do you handle them?
   •   What has been the most satisfying achievement in your career to date?
   •   What are the three most important skills that you have developed in your career so far?

   Search also relates to the future:

   •   Why do you think you can be effective after the acquisition?
   •   Which of your qualifications and experiences do you feel are most relevant?
   •   What do you not have that you think will be needed?

4   Probe – used to dig deeper, when the interviewer is not sure that what has been heard is correct or complete. Probe is also used to counter evasion:

   •   Can we just go over that once again?
   •   I am sorry, but I must be clear on this one. Why exactly did you do that?
   •   We seem to have wandered off the subject.

Effective probing can also be silent or near silent. A nod of the head, an 'I see' or 'go on' or a slightly raised eyebrow may be all that is needed to dig deeper

5   Check – to check that the interviewer has understood correctly. The most effective means of checking is to paraphrase what the interviewee has just said. Another is to ask the same question some time later

Body language

Answers to questions do not tell everything. Body language can often tell a lot more and, because it is hard to disguise, it can often be nearer the truth. For these reasons, it is important to be on the lookout for subtle, spontaneous, reactions. Few interviewees at this level will blush, but many will look away or at their shoes when not wholly convinced by the answer they have given.

The conclusion

It is important that the interview ends with both sides feeling it has been a worthwhile exercise. In particular, interviewees should not be left feeling that there has not been a proper opportunity to say everything that they feel needs saying or that they have been denied the opportunity of selling themselves. The interviewer, as controller of the process, can avoid a sense of dissatisfaction by winding down the interview in a slow, premeditated way by saving some of the easier questions for the winding down, signalling clearly that the end is in sight and asking if there is anything else the respondent wants to cover.

Psychometric tests

Psychometric tests quantify personality. Personality, like ability, is a key influence on performance. It is also the key to building a balanced team.

Psychometric tests use self-reporting questionnaires. These ask about preferred ways of behaving and of relating to other people. Carrying out psychometric tests properly and professionally means either consulting a chartered occupational psychologist or passing a prescribed training course. Reputable publishers will not supply tests unless the person carrying them out is suitably qualified.

Although there are many different forms of personality questionnaire, they all tend to fall in to one of two psychological camps

*   Type. These assign the respondent to a specific personality type
*   Trait. These categorise according to personality trait, where a trait is an aspect of personality which the respondent possesses to a greater or lesser extent

Personality type

By far the most widely used type of questionnaire is the *Myers-Briggs Type Indicator®* (*MBTI®*). At their most basic, they categorise human behaviour into four base types, hence the term 'four quadrant behaviour' (4QB), although many of the commercially available tests go well beyond this, breaking the basic four types into many more sub-types.

As far as management assessments are concerned, questionnaires like the *MBTI®* can provide considerable insight into the way a person interrelates with others, their preferred role in group situations and their favoured work environment. This can help understand the strengths and weaknesses of a team.

Personality traits

Trait questionnaires measure the different amounts of personality characteristics which we all possess. The theory is that the traits are predictive of behaviour. Two of the most commonly used psychological tests in the UK are 16PF (Sixteen Personality Factor Questionnaire), which measures sixteen personality traits, and the Occupational Personality Questionnaire® (OPQ®), which measures thirty.

Management referencing

Even if they do not feel the need for full-blown management appraisals, many acquirers need to satisfy themselves on the background and integrity of management teams. In these circumstances, they are likely to require some management referencing. The process is as follows.

A CV provides the basic background information of the individuals concerned. The next phase seeks to expand and verify the information contained in the CV. This is done through a mixture of desk research and primary information sources. Typically, due diligence investigations will cover:

- Confirmation that the manager lives at the address claimed. Brief assessment of the residence
- Credit reference check. Any county court judgements or other bad credit associated with either the person or the address?
- Media checks. Are there any past articles which may cause concern?
- Verification of qualifications and job history
- Past experience check. Interviews with previous employers to confirm information on the CV (dates, remuneration, responsibilities, etc.),

reasons for leaving and to try to elicit any information on past performance and character
- Verification of professional memberships
- Industry enquiries. To try to establish whether there is anything in the
  manager's background which might cause concern. Is the individual
  seen as competent, honest and respected? Ex-colleagues can be particularly revealing sources
- A list of current directorships and shareholdings

Reporting

Reports should give an insight into individual managers and into the capabilities of the senior management team as a team. They should contain the
following.

For individuals, an executive summary on each of the key managers
assessed, which:

- Profiles their capabilities against a broad range of general management
  competencies
- Matches these against the managerial challenges that will need to be
  addressed over the next few years
- Highlights their strengths and weaknesses
- Benchmarks them against senior managers in other organisations
- Indicates what areas of development or support would compensate for
  the weaknesses
- Provides the behavioural evidence to back up these conclusions

For the team, or proposed team, a profile which:

- Maps out the overall strengths and weaknesses of the management
  team as a whole
- Identifies where individuals' strengths complement each other
- Exposes any specific experience or capability that may be lacking in
  the team

Reporting will be against some or all of the following nine attributes,
although more detail may be sought depending on the nature of the acquisition and its integration.

- Strategic vision. The degree to which the candidate is able to formulate
  and articulate a vision of the business several years down the road

- Leadership/communication. Ability to build and motivate teams, set goals and objectives, guide staff towards them and confront any performance problems
- Customer and market orientation. Empathy with customers and the needs of the market place. Ability to respond to and anticipate change and be able to build the same customer/market dedication in the staff
- Teamwork
- Performance orientation. Evidence of delivering, for example, profit or sales growth (or both) and a personality which sets and communicates firm business goals and tracks performance against them
- Functional capability. This usually boils down to technical if the candidate is a professional such as a finance director
- Change orientation
- Energy and resilience. Evidence of drive, stamina, hard work and resilience
- Ability to deal with pressure. Candidates can cope with stress and are not uncomfortable with ambiguity and complexity

Post-acquisition planning

It is one thing to decide which managers or groups of employees are key. It is quite another to retain them once the deal is done. Before negotiations have even finished, employees start to become anxious. Ideally, therefore, key employees should learn of their fate well before due diligence ends. Very often, there is no substitute for cash, not just to retain employees, but also to ensure their performance through the uncertainty of the negotiation period. Retention incentives add 5 to 10 per cent to the total cost of a deal, which is enough to wreck it. It is therefore vital to anticipate them. Once quantified, the cost of retention incentives can be fed into the valuation model just like all the other due diligence findings.

Conclusion

The right management is critical to the success of a deal. It must make sense, therefore, to consider management appraisals in the due diligence programme. The objective is to assess management's capability, both as individuals and as a team, in the context of what needs to be achieved post-acquisition. The approach places most weight on past-orientated interviews, but supplements these with other types of interview and possibly also psychometric tests. A human resources professional should be able to benchmark the target management against managers in similar positions, with similar challenges, in other organisations. It should also identify employees who are key to the business, which in turn means that the costs of retaining key employees can be anticipated while the deal is still being negotiated.

9 Pensions due diligence

Pensions can be a significant concern in acquisitions and must be taken into account at an early stage since they may affect decisions as to both the price and the structure of the transaction.

If you acquire a UK company, you could encounter one of three common types of pension arrangement:

*   A group personal pension plan (GPPP)
*   A defined contribution (DC) pension scheme
*   A defined benefit (DB) pension scheme

With a GPPP or a DC pension scheme, the employer's liability is mostly limited to paying the contributions on time. The main due diligence questions will be to confirm that they have been paid and then the pension's role in employee benefits and employee motivation.

With a DB pension scheme, the employee is told what pension he should get. It is provided by a scheme set up under trust. The following relates to DB schemes only.

A DB pension scheme attaches to the sole or principal employer (often the top company in a group). If you acquire shares in the principal employer, the scheme comes too. It is not usually possible to segregate the liabilities for active employees from the pensions of former employees. The pension scheme could quite easily be worth more than the company being bought.

The employer meets the bulk of the cost. Contributions are determined by the scheme's rules and overriding law. The scheme rules might give the power to set contribution rates to the trustees, the employer or the scheme actuary.

An employer cannot just walk away from its pension obligations. If an employer winds up a DB pension scheme, it is obliged to fund the plan sufficiently to allow the trustees to buy insurance policies to cover all pension liabilities. These will cost a lot – much more than the accounting liabilities.

DB pension scheme assets and liabilities are valued differently for different purposes. For this reason, a pension scheme may be underfunded on one valuation basis and overfunded on another.

- Trustees will use a "going concern" basis. This assumes salaries continue to grow and pensions are paid from the scheme.
- UK statute currently imposes Scheme Specific Funding Requirements (SSFR). Under SSFR, private sector DB schemes are required to have a valuation every three years. Schemes showing a deficit must put in place a recovery plan and send this to the Pensions Regulator (TPR) for review within 15 months. Both valuation and recovery plan must be 'scheme specific', with assumptions depending on the circumstances of each scheme. Trustees should aim for any funding shortfall to be eliminated as quickly as the employer can reasonably afford.
- 'Discontinuance' and 'buy-out' look at liabilities on winding up and are similar: the estimated and the actual cost of securing all liabilities with annuities – the most conservative bases.

Section 28 of FRS 102 attempts to recognise the funding position of the scheme in the employer's accounts. It is not linked to the real funding requirements of the scheme or the employer's ultimate liability.

If an acquisition does not involve all the companies within a group, it is likely that any group pension plan will remain with the seller. In these circumstances, the target company will usually leave the plan on the sale, resulting in its share of the annuitised liability to the pension plan becoming immediately payable. This cost can be significant.

The UK Pensions Regulator also has to be factored in. It has the power in a number of circumstances to bring a direction against any group company, requiring it to fund a defined benefit pension plan. For example, it can take action where it believes:

- The plan sponsor is insufficiently resourced to meet its pension liabilities.
- An act or failure to act has detrimentally affected the likelihood of accrued benefits being received in a material way.
- A transaction is intended to reduce the chances of a pension liability being paid in full.

A buyer with fewer assets or a lower credit rating than the seller may be at risk of such a claim.

To limit the risk of regulatory intervention, it is common practice for the buyer to seek clearance from the Pensions Regulator as a condition of closing. Sellers may be reluctant to agree to clearance because:

- The Pensions Regulator often asks for a payment into the plan, which is usually deducted from the purchase price.
- If clearance is applied for but not granted, the sale may not go through and the seller has simply alerted the Pensions Regulator to potential problems in its pension plan.

Clearance can be time-consuming, involving the Pensions Regulator canvassing the views of the plan trustees. Obtaining the agreement of both the trustees and the Pensions Regulator can take several weeks.

Given the above, the biggest concern will be funding deficits. Other issues will include

- Whether there are major claims against the scheme(s)
- Whether or not the buyer is inheriting pension promises outside the terms of the approved company scheme. For example, highly paid employees often have a contractual promise that they will be paid a pension based on their full salary, with any excess over the pensions cap paid by the employing company. (UK tax authorities impose a limit on the tax relief for pension contributions)
- Whether the acquired scheme is to be merged with existing schemes. If not, does the buyer wish to 'red circle' the acquired schemes so that no new employees join it?
- Is the purchaser happy to continue providing defined benefits (e.g. where pension is linked to number of years in the scheme and final salary) or does it wish to move to money purchase schemes?
- Whether it is happy to provide a company pension at all, or whether it wants to move to personal pension schemes
- If the buyer has inherited a non-contributory scheme (i.e. where only the employer contributes), does it want to introduce employee contributions?

With an asset purchase, you normally do not get the scheme, but you may still get pension liabilities. While no occupational pension rights will automatically transfer, if an employee has the right to an employer contribution paid into a personal pension scheme, this obligation transfers to the buyer.

The actuary

A buyer cannot rely on the seller's assessment of future liabilities and will normally use an actuary to carry out the due diligence on pension arrangements and to advise on negotiations. Unfortunately, in addition to the different calculation methods listed above, final pensionable pay and investment returns are both unknown and need to be projected using actuarial assumptions. Those assumptions can have a huge impact on the final number and should, therefore, be carefully negotiated, as should the outcome of the actuaries work. Should, for example, a surplus be added to the price? (Not if it cannot be realised – although the seller will argue differently.)

What, precisely, the actuary will do depends on the nature of the transaction.

Whole scheme

If the deal involves taking over an entire pension scheme, the actuary will:

• Value the scheme; that is, it will assess the scheme's ability to meet expected liabilities. Valuation involves a myriad of assumptions
• Ensure statutory requirements, such as equal pay, have been provided for
• Advise on any unfunded promises
• Advise on any creative accounting involving pensions

Bulk transfer

If the deal involves taking a transfer from the seller's scheme, the actuary will:

• Negotiate the size of the transfer and its terms and conditions
• Advise on the cost implications of an inadequate transfer
• Advise on any creative accounting (as above)

Information

Early on, the actuary will need:

• A full list of those transferring along with their employment details. There is an obvious overlap with human resources due diligence here, and the two sets of advisers must talk to each other
• For each scheme from which employees are transferring:

    • The Trust Deed and Rules
    • Member's handbook
    • Announcements made since both of the above were last updated

- Confirmation that equal pay and increases are provided for
- Latest actuarial report/review

- Information on any unfunded pension commitments, both approved and unapproved
- Verification that the required approvals have been obtained
- Whether there is any regulatory interest

Warranties and indemnities

Trustees run occupational pension schemes, and trustees are not bound by any action that is in breach of trust. To be worth anything, indemnities must, therefore, be given by the vendor. Particular issues to watch out for are:

- Unfunded pension promises. A warranty to deal with unfunded liabilities is always advisable
- Where buying a company with an insured-style occupational pension scheme, and if valuation is to be carried out post-completion, the purchaser can *try* to obtain an indemnity from the vendor to cover the possibility that the insurance policy backing the scheme is enough to meet the liabilities. This, however, is unlikely to be given, and in any case opens the seller to the risk that the vendor will want a similar *quid pro quo* if there proves to be a surplus
- A purchaser needs to be certain that if a vendor's scheme cannot pay the agreed transfer amount, then the vendor will make up the shortfall

Conclusion

The importance, and nature, of pensions due diligence depends partly on the target's existing pension arrangements and partly on what the purchaser is intending post transaction. If the target has a defined benefits occupational pension scheme, then the size of the financial risk makes close scrutiny of the funding of future pension liabilities a must. This is a complex, highly technical area which can be further complicated by the type of transaction, whether or not the target's employees are coming out of a larger scheme and the attitude of pension fund trustees, so it pays to use a good actuary with whom you can work. The actuary can also advise on post-acquisition planning. If, on the other hand, the target company has a defined contribution scheme, or employees are contributing to personal pensions, funding is less of an issue, but there may be employee relations issues which have to be addressed.

10 Tax due diligence

Tax due diligence is about both risk and opportunity. The challenge is to keep the tax advisers focused on the commercial picture. Anglo-Saxon practice is for there to be a tax indemnity. This means that the seller will pay any pre-deal tax which falls due after the deal is done. In practice, indemnities are not fail-safe, which is why buyers carry out tax due diligence. The tax deed should be seen as a backstop and not as a prime means of avoiding risk:

- An indemnity is only as good as the person giving it
- Indemnities have time limits and contain *de minimus* provisions
- Past liabilities are only part of the story. The transaction itself might trigger liabilities

Tax overlaps with both legal and financial due diligence, which means that whoever is working on tax must liaise closely with the financial and legal advisers to ensure that information is properly shared, that nothing falls between the cracks and that there is no duplication of effort.

Although corporate taxes are the ones that grab all the attention, it is the other taxes which are likely to be the most troublesome.

Objectives

The objectives of tax due diligence are threefold.

- To find and protect against tax exposures which are not reflected in the purchase price
- To plan for tax issues which will arise as a result of the deal
- To structure the deal in the most tax efficient manner

Transaction related tax due diligence

The principal taxes to be considered are:

- Corporate taxes
- VAT/sales taxes
- Employment taxes such as income tax, payroll taxes and other deductions
- Employee benefit reporting
- Stamp duties, transfer duties and capital duties on the acquisition

The target's shareholders' personal taxes may also be of interest, especially those which may be charged to the target company, such as inheritance taxes, estate duties and gift taxes. If the acquisition is of assets, only Stamp Duty and VAT are relevant. Both are levied on the transaction itself and easily identified. The higher the asset value, the more the tax, which is another reason for not taking over debtors.

Activities

The main activities involved can be summarised as follows:

- Review of corporate tax returns and computations
- Review of correspondence with tax authorities and the status of agreements on outstanding computations
- Details of any inland revenue investigations and of tax audits by foreign tax authorities
- Analysis of corporate tax and deferred tax provisions in financial statements
- Review of quarterly payment procedures

Briefing advisers

Specifics of the tax investigation will include:

- Materiality levels
- The companies to be investigated. This is only an issue where the acquisition is being made from a group of companies. If it sounds odd to suggest that the tax advisers should be instructed to investigate companies other than the target, the reason is that some tax authorities, and HMRC in the UK is one of them, have the power in certain circumstances to

collect tax from a company which has in the past been in the same group as a defaulting company
- The time period to be covered. In the UK, there is a statutory limitation period of six years for non-fraud cases, which means that any tax returns more than six years old cannot be reopened and reinvestigated. Usual practice is to review the previous three years and then take a view on going back further
- Taxes to be covered. There may be specialist taxes, depending on the industry
- Areas of risk specific to the transaction. If, for example, the target has aggressively managed tax in the past, what are the chances of the purchaser becoming liable? Other possible concerns are listed below under 'common areas of concern'

The buyer's advisers should understand the seller's, as well as the buyer's, tax situation. It is frequently possible to structure the deal to minimise overall tax liabilities. Saving tax for the seller ought to be tradable, either directly as money off the purchase price or in exchange for some other contentious issue which comes up in negotiations.

Information sources

Data rooms

Data rooms are unlikely to give more than a rough outline of the target's tax history. Sometimes there are a lot of detailed calculations but no explanation; at other times the tax levied will be split by business, but there will be no geographical split. Furthermore, although it may well be possible to identify and quantify specific exposures, it is often difficult to see whether a provision has been made for them in the accounts.

Nonetheless, it is worth the tax adviser visiting the data room, not only to review the documents on tax, but also to have a look at the basic company documents. What shares have been issued, and what rights attach to them? Have there been any repayments of capital which could count as a distribution? Are they ordinary shares? Who are the registered shareholders (and therefore who will be giving warranty and indemnity protection)? Is there anything, such as owners being resident abroad, which suggests extra protection might be needed in the event of a breach of warranty? Are there any shareholder agreements, especially ones which govern control of the target? If so, do these have a bearing on group structure? What is the group structure – and, just as important, is this the structure that the seller's tax advisers or tax department is working to? It sounds obvious, but it is well worth the tax advisers drawing up their understanding of the group structure and confirming it with the seller.

It is surprising just how often the seller's company secretary, tax and treasury departments all work to different group structures.

Risk profile

At an early stage in the during tax diligence exercise, a useful piece of analysis is to build up a profile of the target's risk profile. Table 10.1 highlights the sources of tax risk:

The risk profile should give the tax adviser a reliable feel for the priorities and therefore avoid getting into too much unnecessary detail.

Tax warranties

The next step is a list of questions for the vendor. With tax, these questions usually take the form of warranties for the seller to disclose against,

Table 10.1 Profiling the tax risk in target companies

	Low tax risk	*Medium tax risk*	*High tax risk*
• Deal structure	• Assets based	• Share based	• Share based
• Company type	• Single company	• Multi-company	• Multi-company
• Company business	• Simple	• Complex	• Specialist sector
• Span of operations	• Wholly domestic	• Some overseas operations	• Substantial overseas operations
• Tax rate	• Losses (which are not being paid for)/tax rate close to standard	• Tax rate below what it should be	• Low effective tax rate
• Tax planning	• None	• Some evidence of tax planning	• Evidence of aggressive tax planning
• Compliance	• No issues	• Moderate compliance arrears	• Heavy compliance arrears
• Tax audits	• Recent clean tax audits	• Recent tax audits	• No recent tax audits
• Disputes with the Revenue	• No items under dispute	• Few items under dispute	• Many items under dispute
• Transfer pricing	• Not an issue	• Policy in place	• No documentation
• Length of time in business	• Recent start up	• Long trading history	• Long trading history

ideally followed by face-to-face meetings. The principal role of tax warranties is to find things out rather than to put the seller on the hook. This being the case, it is very important to make sure that disclosures are not vague or incomplete. Oral disclosures should be resisted, as should general statements. The tax adviser will want to know not just that certain transactions took place, but will need details and copies of any supporting documentation.

In all cases, additional warranties will be drawn up at the end of the process to elicit information on any areas of uncertainty or where the position needs clarifying.

A seller may resist disclosing against certain warranties on the grounds that the tax authorities might want to see disclosure letters. Such a claim should put the buyer on the alert for potentially un-provided tax liabilities.

Areas of interest

Depending on the exact nature of the transaction, there are a number of areas for each type of tax which are likely to be of most concern. These are covered in the following sections, starting with corporate taxes.

Corporate taxes

COMPLIANCE RECORD

A company's compliance record is a good guide to how it will be treated by the tax authorities. A poor record and you can almost guarantee that that the authorities will look very carefully at everything a company submits.

In the UK, a company is required to:

- Calculate its own liability for corporation tax
- File a return by the filing date (twelve months after the year-end)
- Pay the tax it has calculated
- Keep records for six years

HMRC:

- Has up to twelve months from filing to launch an inquiry into a return
- Will issue a closure notice once an inquiry has been resolved

Checking whether or not self-assessment returns have been correctly submitted is an important element of tax due diligence on UK companies.

PAST TRANSACTIONS

The tax adviser is particularly interested in anything which might be a potential exposure, but which has not been provided for. Some of the biggest potential exposures lie with tax avoidance schemes, and especially ones which have yet to be examined by the tax authorities.

Another risk lies with past M&A transactions where the target may have given or received tax warranties and indemnities. These should also be reviewed and the risk of crystallisation assessed.

THE STATUS OF CURRENT TAX NEGOTIATIONS

Once the deal is done, the purchaser will be responsible for tax compliance. The purchaser needs to ensure:

*   A smooth transition. The purchaser will need to find out where tax negotiations with the authorities have got to and which matters it will have to take up once the target is under new ownership
*   That there are no disputes over computations. The most common areas are:

    *   Capital allowance claims and bad debt provisions
    *   Un-agreed valuations (which could have an impact on capital gains liabilities)
    *   Outstanding transfer pricing disputes

*   That claims and elections are made within statutory time limits. Time limits could easily expire while the deal is being negotiated
*   That, if consent has been given for a joint claim or election, this cannot be withdrawn

Often special agreements are made with the tax authorities, and it is important to understand what these are and whether they will continue.

GROUP TRANSACTIONS

If the target is a member of a group, there may be some particular risks which need to be covered:

*   There may have been inter-group transfers which give rise to de-grouping charges on capital gains once the deal is done
*   There may be a similar issue with intra-group Stamp Duty relief

- The buyer may need to understand the system for group and consortium relief surrenders and whether any inter-group payments are outstanding
- Whether the target is liable for any taxes of the group companies not acquired. For example, if transfer prices could are judged not to be have been at arm's length

THE AVAILABILITY OF TAX LOSSES

Tax losses can be extremely important to the viability of a transaction. The reality is that they can easily be lost. Avoid paying for tax losses unless and until you use them.

Cross-border acquisitions

TRANSFER PRICING

Transfer pricing is a mechanism which is used as a means of reducing tax. Transfer prices based on arms-length relationships using market prices will satisfy the tax man. In practice, 'market prices' are notoriously difficult to show. Transfer pricing risk is especially significant in cross-border acquisitions. Due diligence should determine the target's exposure to transfer pricing adjustments and any likely tax liabilities. This will include an examination of the transfer pricing policy of the group of which the target is a member, and an assessment of how that policy has been implemented across the group.

TAX CLEARANCES REQUIRED FOR THE TRANSACTION

Certain clearances may be needed for the transaction to go ahead. The purchaser should make sure they:

- Have been applied for
- Have been properly drafted
- Are submitted in good time

VAT/sales taxes and customs duties

The first, and crucial, VAT question is whether the target is registered for VAT. If it is not, should it be, and if so, have any measures been taken to rectify the lack of registration?

Assuming the target is VAT registered, the tax adviser will examine VAT returns for the past two years to make sure it has been properly accounted for. Particular issues which should be checked, and reported on, are whether:

- Returns been correctly filed within the correct time limits
- Tax has been paid on time and, if not, whether interest, or any other penalty, has been adequately provided for
- The accounting systems are adequate to produce monthly returns
- Disputes are likely with Customs and Excise
- The target is a member of a VAT group. If so, it will be jointly and severally liable for the liabilities of other group members. The buyer needs contractual protection against any such outstanding VAT liabilities

The VAT treatment of the actual acquisition also needs careful consideration. Any mistake here and one party or the other might find itself liable for VAT on the entire consideration.

Employment taxes

The principles that apply to employment taxes are similar to those that apply to VAT:

- Have the relevant taxes been correctly deducted and paid over on time? This may sound fairly obvious, but could be an issue if there are contractors paid on invoice. Directors' benefits are always an area of concern
- What dispensations or special arrangements have been agreed with the revenue? Will they survive the transaction?
- Have there been any enquiries by any of the relevant authorities? If so, what was their outcome? Are they finished? Are the same matters likely to arise in the future?
- Are there any share schemes or profit related pay schemes? If so:
  - What are the rules?
  - Has the Revenue approved them?
  - How will they be affected by the transaction?

Other taxes

- Stamp duty should not be passed over. The tax adviser should review any outstanding liabilities and any impact the transaction might have

on the buyer's stamp duty position, although the main effort is likely to go into minimising stamp duty on the transaction itself.
- Customs duties should not be forgotten, if relevant. Tax due diligence needs to confirm that customs duties have been correctly calculated and that there are no outstanding issues from any customs audits

Transaction related tax planning

As a very minimum, the buyer needs:

- Access to any records, correspondence *and people* that may be needed in post-acquisition negotiations with the tax authorities
- To agree who should be responsible for resolving outstanding issues with the tax authorities. This needs careful thought because if the (tax indemnified) buyer is in charge, will it settle too easily? On the other hand, if the seller is to agree outstanding issues, how hard will it fight if it thinks the tax will be picked up by buyer?

Integration related tax planning

Where the acquirer has operations in the same territory, there are generally tax benefits to be had from creating a single tax grouping by merging the target with existing operations. This may give rise to capital gains problems.

The target will also need to be integrated in the most tax efficient way. It may be that some of the target's assets are to be sold. The investigation should aim to identify how best the target can be integrated, e.g. which company in the acquiring group should buy it and whether any liabilities are going to be triggered by reorganisations.

Structuring

Post-acquisition planning becomes even more important with international acquisitions. It pays to acquire foreign companies with the right place. You do not want to be moving them around once they have been acquired. This in turn may require the co-operation of the seller, who may not be too keen to reorganise at the same time as trying to get the deal done.

For all buyers, the most important structuring objectives are likely to be:

- Avoiding double taxation
- Maximising relief for interest on borrowed funds
- Minimising withholding taxes
- Obtaining a step up of assets for depreciation purposes
- Obtaining relief for acquisition costs

This in turn means that it is difficult to separate the tax aspects of the transaction itself from the longer-term post-completion tax planning.

Each of the above points is dealt with in turn below.

Double taxation

A company resident in the UK will generally be liable for UK corporation tax on its income from all sources worldwide. It may also be liable for overseas tax on income which falls within the tax net of other countries. Also, dividends and interest paid by overseas companies to UK shareholders may have suffered withholding tax in the country of origin and then be taxable again in the UK. Double Tax Relief (DTR) exists to reduce that tax burden. It ensures that the taxpayer pays no more than the higher of the two rates involved. DTR is given according to the terms of double tax agreements which the UK has entered into with most countries in the world.

Maximising interest relief

The single most important reason why tax advisers need to be involved with structuring the transaction is because most acquisitions will be financed at least partly by debt; the financial success of the deal will be profoundly influenced by how much tax relief can be claimed for the interest on that debt. As interest is tax deductible in all the main trading nations, the trick is to ensure that interest is borne in a jurisdiction where profits are being taxed at a high effective rate. Locating debt in those countries where there are taxable profits against which can be offset is called 'debt pushdown'.

The effectiveness of debt pushdown will depend on four things:

- Vendor structure. It is much easier to push debt down if the vendor is selling lots of separate companies
- Where the profits are made. In the absence of other data, the historical earnings split is a good guide to where profits might be made in the future
- Allocation of purchase price. The amount of the purchase price allocated to a country will determine how much debt can be pushed down to that country. The vendor is will have its own ideas on this, which may complicate the planning
- Limitations imposed by tax rules in each of the relevant counties

  - The ability to offset interest against trading profits
  - Limitations on the amount of intra-group debt (or thin capitalisation, see below)
  - Withholding taxes on interest payments

The mechanics of debt pushdown are simple. A Newco in a country acquires the target in the same country. The idea is that the interest Newco has to pay on the loans needed to buy the target can be offset against the profits which the target makes. Most countries' tax rules allow this – although in some jurisdictions some form of post-acquisition merger may be required to make it work.

THIN CAPITALISATION

In order to prevent taxable profits being eliminated by the use of acquisition debt, most countries have rules which restrict the amount of related party debt which can be used in a company's capital structure. The rules vary enormously from country to country. Thin capitalisation is often negotiated with the tax authorities on a case-by-case basis.

Withholding taxes on dividends

Withholding taxes on dividends can be a significant levy on the repatriation of profits. These withholding taxes are reduced under double tax relief.

Step ups

If assets can be stepped up to their market values for tax purposes, then there will be a tax saving. The good news is that most countries grant a step up where assets are acquired, and most (the UK is an exception) will allow depreciation of intangibles as well as tangibles. There are also a limited number of countries where a step up is available for tax depreciable assets where the shares of the target are acquired.

Obtaining relief for acquisition costs

This is a specialist area. Money spent on a good tax adviser is money well spent. Here it is necessary only to be aware that there are a number of ways of getting relief for acquisition costs. One, for example, is to split intangible assets from the acquired company, then lease them back to the new acquisition, sheltering the resulting lease charges in a low tax regime. In this way, the purchaser can get a deduction against highly taxed profits and receipts in a low tax jurisdiction. Due diligence tax advisers should be encouraged to report on the options in this area.

Conclusion

Although in Anglo-Saxon jurisdictions sellers will give a tax indemnity, the principle of *caveat emptor* makes it advisable for buyers to make their own enquiries into the tax risks of a transaction. But tax due diligence should not be restricted to the transaction. It can also play a valuable role in post-acquisition structuring.

Corporate taxes are the usual focus, but the biggest risk can often lie with the other corporate taxes. Data rooms and disclosures against tax warranties are valuable information sources but, as with other forms of due diligence, there is no substitute for direct access. Cross-border acquisitions introduce an extra layer of complexity, both for the transaction and for tax planning. Local advice should be taken on transaction related tax issues, and advisers should be encouraged to report on any tax planning opportunities.

Taxation is a highly technical, complex and ever changing discipline. To be done properly, it needs to be carried out by experts. However, the potential size of liabilities which could be acquired, or of the savings which are available if the deal is most effectively structured, can make tax due diligence a rewarding area.

11 Environmental due diligence

Environmental due diligence is not just about contaminated land and chimneys belching out acrid smoke. Just as important are operational liabilities. If a target business is not complying with the relevant legislation, for example, a buyer could find itself landed with a substantial capital programme.

Objectives

Environmental due diligence has two strands. These are identifying and quantifying:

- Environmental risks which would be inherited. A potential liability for cleaning up contaminated land would be a good example
- The costs of meeting any continuing obligations, for example upgrading equipment and procedures. This could be a big item where there has been significant non-compliance with environmental regulations

The focus will probably be on some or all of the following areas:

- The nature and extent of any land contamination
- The presence of substances which may cause contamination in future
- The degree of compliance with environmental regulation
- Environmental management

Process

As with other types of due diligence, the starting question is do I have to carry out environmental due diligence, and if so, how much? The answer may be "not much" – the seller may have told the buyer everything it needs to know. The more information the seller gives the buyer, the more likely the seller can escape liability. When it comes to contaminated land, if the seller tells the buyer everything, the buyer is 'buying with knowledge' and any liability is transferred. As far as the buyer is concerned, this means treating the results of environmental due diligence extremely carefully. It could easily result in liabilities transferring to the buyer which might otherwise have remained with the seller.

Advisers

Assuming, though, that a buyer does require some due diligence, the question is who to commission to carry it out. Unlike solicitors and accountants, there is no governing body for environmental consultancies. References and recommendations are, therefore, doubly essential.

Once a suitable consultancy has been selected, watch out for the consultant's standard terms of appointment. These are usually drafted to minimise their financial exposure to negligence. Check insurance cover as well. This is very important where there are likely to be Phase 2 enquiries, because the Phase 2 work itself could cause damage.

Cross-border considerations

Every jurisdiction is different. Each site in each jurisdiction must be treated on its own merits, and the findings viewed against local legislation. However, it is also important for the overall investigation that risk is assessed in a consistent manner. What is needed is local investigation and local interpretation, but a central risk assessment methodology.

Land contamination

Land contamination and clean-up costs will be a concern in many deals. Traditionally, this is a two-stage process:

- Phase 1 review, which is a review of existing knowledge, public data and other information on the target to identify any areas of concern
- Phase 2 review, which are the intrusive enquiries required to monitor, sample and fully analyse any concerns raised in Phase 1. Each site is unique, and the work will be site specific

Information sources

Desk research

The first step is usually a desktop study, with the consultants trawling through relevant information sources to weigh up the chances of the land or surrounding area being contaminated. At the same time, they would examine:

- The physical characteristics of the area – the hydrology and geology, for example
- The economic context – for example, land use
- Records of statutory bodies to identify anything which could be on the receiving end of pollution, such as boreholes and rivers. As pollution can travel, environmental consultants should always to be thinking not just in terms of what contaminants might be present, but also the likelihood of them travelling and having an impact on a wider area

This assessment will set the scene for any Phase 2 work.

Data rooms

If there is a data room involved in a transaction, a lot of this data should be in there. Data rooms will usually contain some or all of the following:

- Environmental consultants' reports
- Environmental policies
- Lists of any hazardous materials kept on site
- Details of accidents and spillages
- Details of breaches of consents
- Enforcement notices (following environmental damage or breach of compliance)

Management information

When reviewing management information, it is worth bearing in mind what is in place now, and what the position will be once the deal is done. If the target is part of a bigger company which has been able to rely on corporate resources, there may be a cost to be factored into the deal which reflects the cost of no longer being able to draw on the parent's corporate environmental organisation.

Regulatory authorities

In the UK, regulatory authorities such as the Environment Agency and the Local Authority will be able to provide authorisations, permits and licences, and also details of any enforcements. The local water company will have details of consents to carry out any trade effluent discharges.

A Phase 1 study can obtain a lot of useful information by talking to the regulatory authorities. As is the case with tax, past relationships with the authorities can be a good indication of how they are likely to treat a site or company in the future.

Site visits

Following the initial desk research come visits to those sites where possible material issues have been identified. The objective is not to carry out detailed drilling or sampling, but to see the site and see how operations are carried out. The environmental auditor will aim to:

- Further assess the nature and extent of any contamination through interviews with relevant site personnel and reviewing existing site studies
- Audit the presence of hazardous materials and their packaging, handling, distribution and containment
- Review permits and licences and understand the degree of compliance with environmental regulations
- Audit the effectiveness of environmental management

Phase 1 conclusions

At this stage, it should be possible to come to a view on whether there are any environmental issues which will have an impact on the deal. If there are potentially serious issues which require further investigation, a buyer might have to commission a 'Phase 2' investigation.

Phase 2 investigations

Phase 2 work can be costly, risky and take a long time. The work will probably involve sampling the soil and groundwater and analysing the samples in a laboratory. It may be done in stages. It is something best left to experts adept at identifying contamination 'hotspots' and skilled at not unduly disturbing contamination during their enquiries. The last thing needed is for the enquiries themselves to give rise to liabilities. Because of this very risk, sellers sometimes resist Phase 2 audits. Often, only the negotiation of extensive indemnities will persuade them to grant access.

Reporting

The report should permit the purchaser to evaluate the environmental risk. This is not just a question of dealing with the problems identified, but also the costs and other mechanisms needed to deal with compliance in the future.

The final report should contain the following headings:

- A description of the issues identified, for example:

  - Legal and/or policy requirements
  - Areas of significantly bad environmental performance

- An assessment of how management has dealt with them.
- Inefficiencies in current practices
- Non-compliance issues
- Steps required to rectify any concerns, non-compliances, etc.
- Priorities for environmental improvements
- Current and future requirements and an assessment of upgrade requirements
- Possible means of achieving these improvements, together with costs and timescales
- A review of whether any of the above costs have already been accounted for, e.g. through provisions or insurance
- Indemnities needed
- Any other potential risks and the chances of them crystallising

Warranties and indemnities

- It is advisable to commission a survey to establish a benchmark of contamination at or near completion so that there are not arguments later about how much pollution was caused since completion by the buyer's activities on the site and how much is genuinely down to the seller's pre-deal activities
- If an indemnity is not negotiated which provides that the seller will meet the costs incurred by the purchaser in any claim arising from any of the risks previously identified and disclosed, there may be a warranty about compliance with the environmental laws and the obtaining of all necessary permits. The seller will be asked to warrant that it has:

  - Complied with all applicable laws
  - All the permits it needs to carry out the business
  - Is not party to any environmental litigation
  - Not caused any toxic or hazardous release into the environment
  - No obligations to remedy soil at any site

Warranties may be perfectly adequate where environmental problems are limited. Because of the time it can take for environmental problems to manifest themselves, the time periods for warranties and indemnities in the environmental field need to be considerably longer than in most other fields. Five to seven years is typical, but much longer periods are not unknown.

Conclusion

Environmental due diligence is normally structured into two phases, although Phase 2 is not always carried out. The first phase will comprise desk research and site visits. The second phase involves intrusive investigations. Advisers need to be chosen with care, and not just for their technical expertise. Their terms of engagement and levels of insurance cover can be just as important. There are number of standard remedies available to cater for any unexpected risks. Which are used very much depends on the deal and the negotiating strength of the parties involved.

12 IT due diligence

IT is frequently ignored in M&A, which is a little surprising given that it is integral to the running and efficiency of all companies. The usual concern is how best to integrate information systems. While the cost and speed of integration are very important, an acquisition is a prime opportunity to make IT a strategic tool, if it is not one already. Besides, integrating legacy systems is often a waste of time and money.

How much to do

The answer to the perennial question of how much investigation to do in this area is going to be a function of:

- What the intentions are post-acquisition
- The importance of information technology

The costs of merging IT systems can be colossal, and the cost savings are usually over-estimated. Unless the target's systems are woefully out of date, it should be possible to get adequate management information out of them. Most systems these days will work alongside each other reasonably well.

If, on the other hand, information technology is a fundamental element of competitive advantage, then due diligence has a different importance.

Investigations

The most common research techniques are:

- Management and staff interviews
- A review of documentation relating to IT practices

Because an acquisition presents the ideal opportunity to re-invent what has gone before and so leapfrog existing strategies, investigations should take place on three levels:

• The audit level. What equipment and software is there? Is it secure? Does it work? Who owns it? What are the outstanding commitments?
• The management level. How well does IT and technology support the business?
• The strategic level. Is the technology and organisation sufficient for the future?

The audit level

Investigation at the 'audit' level is just that. It will do little more than investigate the risks. These are fairly generic and are set out in Figure 12.1:

Vulnerability

Vulnerability is a function of how many users there are and the access controls. There are two ways of accessing a system, physically and electronically. An audit will test the controls around both.

Trust

The level of trust is defined by two factors:

• The level of confidence one can have in the employees
• The trust management have in the system based on their past experience

Complexity

As can be seen from Figure 12.1, complexity has three elements to it.

THE COMPLEXITY OF THE SYSTEM

The higher the integration, the higher the risk. If one function fails, the whole system goes down.

THE NUMBER OF DEPARTMENTS USING THE SYSTEM

For the same reasons, the more departments that rely on a system, the higher the risk. If the system goes down, the whole company goes down.

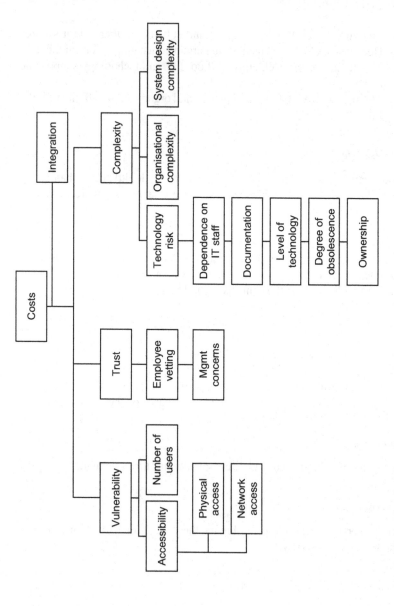

Figure 12.1 Typical subject headings for an IT due diligence audit

THE RISK FROM TECHNOLOGY

The risk from technology is possibly the most pertinent for due diligence. It covers a number of areas:

- The degree of dependence on a small number of key people
- The quality of system documentation
- The level of technology
- The degree of equipment obsolescence
- Ownership, particularly of software. Is it inside or outside the company?

DEPENDENCE ON A FEW KEY IT STAFF

Dependence on a few key IT staff is a critical issue. Acquisitions create uncertainty amongst employees and IT skills are transferable and in short supply.

Dependency risk will be compounded by any negative feelings IT staff have towards the buyer. Minor differences in the way things are done or about future roles can grow into major turf wars, or even sabotage, if not managed properly. People issues can be as important as the technical issues.

DOCUMENTATION

Risk will multiply if documentation is sparse or non-existent, especially if it is in the heads of people who fear for their future.

THE LEVEL OF TECHNOLOGY/DEGREE OF EQUIPMENT OBSOLESCENCE

Level of technology and obsolescence are related. On the one hand, the longer the technology has been in place, the lower the technology risk. Above a certain time, though, the greater the risk that it will have to be replaced shortly after acquisition. As well as the capital costs, if hardware is old and fully written off, recent depreciation charges will have been low. Low depreciation is obviously unsustainable if the equipment is to be replaced soon.

With software, the most critical issue is whether the software is custom-ised for the target company. With relatively old, proprietary systems, the software tends to be not very sophisticated. Standardised packages from software companies that are financially stable and have large installed bases are the safest option. This way there is much more likelihood of continuous technical support and regular product enhancements.

OWNERSHIP OF ASSETS

If the target does not own the IT assets it operates – another group company may own the assets or the licence to operate them – some sort of sub-licensing arrangement may be in place. Other questions to ask would be:

- How long do the licences have left?
- Are there any limitations on licenced software, such as the number of 'seats' or the equipment on which it can be used?
- What agreements are in place to ensure that the licensor maintains the software and provides support within acceptable time limits, and what happens if the licensor goes out of business?
- Do restrictions in the software licences prevent the target outsourcing its IT function?

It is useful to see copies of all software licences and other agreements for the use and maintenance of computer systems and computer software.

Management level

Although IT is critical for most businesses, it is frequently seen as an expense to be minimised. A good starting point for this element of the investigation, therefore, is the company-wide attitude to IT. Is it seen as a strong differentiator, an important element of competitive advantage, a necessary evil or a positive hindrance to progress? How interlinked is IT with the wider business? For example, is the target's aim to use technology to create competitive advantage, or is the focus on ad-hoc pieces of automation? The attitude towards the IT team can reveal a lot. At what level is it represented? In many cases, it should be at board level.

Next is an assessment of the IT team. The team's focus should be at the business level rather than the product/customer level, and it should be business driven rather than technology driven. Over specifying hardware and network infrastructure, unnecessary customisation of software packages and poor control of software licencing are all evidence of a poor focus.

User interviews will shed more light. Does the present system support departmental and company objectives? What do the business units and functional heads say about the IT department? Do they say it is helpful to their objectives and responsive to their needs?

The reason for carrying out investigations at this level is to decide whether a major overhaul of the IT systems and personnel will be needed.

Strategic level

The strategic level is about the contribution of technology to the future. It is partly about using technology to create competitive advantage and it is partly about recognising that IT is essential to all successful companies of the future. Due diligence questions will be along the lines of:

• How closely is the IT plan aligned with the overall corporate plan?
• What is the timescale (benefits from IT projects should be delivered in months, not years)?
• How is IT helping the target to respond to rapidly changing circumstances?
• How is IT giving customers added value?

This is not an easy subject area, even without the pressures of an acquisition. Companies tend to devote the bulk of their IT budgets to maintaining systems and infrastructures, and of the relatively small amount spent on development, only about a third actually delivers value.

Conclusion

IT due diligence is not just about the functionality of the target's systems, or about how best to manage information systems in the combined entity. IT due diligence can take place on three levels. At the audit level, a would-be buyer is concerned with checking that the system is secure, that it works and that it will continue to be secure and work after the deal is done. At the management level, due diligence seeks to unearth some of the cultural issues that may have to be tackled post-acquisition to improve short-term business performance. The strategic level investigation starts with the recognition that IT is a major component of competitive advantage. IT due diligence is as much people as about technology and systems.

13 Technology due diligence

The value of technology is its worth in the market place, both now and in the future. Future worth depends on continued development and exploitation, based on understanding and responding to market needs. As harnessing the creativity of people will ultimately bring the market rewards, the human factor is just as important as the technical.

Technical investigations

The technical investigation can follow a checklist; a simplified example is as follows:

Product Architecture

- Design. What the technology do? How does it work? How it is put together?
- Does the technology deliver the required performance?
- Is there a fit with the business plan? Does the technology perform to the standards required by the business plan?
- Scalability. Is the product capable of going from test bed–type applications to full-scale commercial use?
- Robustness. Will the technology and architecture cope with the demands of live commercial operations?
- Quality

Underlying technology

- Stage of development. Where is the underlying technology in life-cycle terms? Is the technology widely developed? Who else uses it and what for? Has it been patented in other countries or by competitors?
- Is the technology indispensable, or are there potential substitutes?
- Is it appropriate to the application, or is it a technophile's solution?

- Can the target deploy the chosen technology?
- How appropriate is the underlying technology for the future, e.g. could it turn out to be a constraint to growth?

Intellectual property (see Chapter 14)

Commercialisation

- Estimates of commercialisation costs
- Complexity of commercialisation
- Are the appropriate skills and systems in place for commercialisation? Do the plans for commercialisation agree with the business plan?
- Are the skills and systems required for market support in place?

Analysis of documentation

- Overall structure. Assessment of overall quality, including consistency and the process by which business objectives are translated into design goals
- Core components. Conceptualisation of product positioning and key intellectual property elements
- Environmental requirements
- Operational documentation

Other questions for the development and technical staff are:

- Do they have enough of the right equipment?
- How good is the communication between development, test and technical support? Do technical support talk to development so that problems in the field are dealt with effectively? Do they share a database of logged faults? Is technical support fully aware of planned new features and other developments?
- Does the company have full rights to all the technology it uses? If any technology or design feature was originated by non-employees, who has the rights (see the next chapter on intellectual property for further details)?
- Are non-disclosure agreements in place for employees and contractors?

Market investigations

Technical appraisal needs to be supplemented by enquiries in the market place and some human resources detective work.

Some fundamental questions can be answered by simple questions like, does the product actually work? Why do customers purchase? What benefits does it deliver? How does it rate against competing products or substitutes?

Technical support can also be critical to product performance, and this will often need checking out in much the same way. Again, talk to customers. What is the response like? What response does the customer want? Is it easy to get to the right person or get an answer?

New product development

Fixing problems and keeping ahead with new releases is another important feature of product technology. Due diligence should, therefore, look at the decision making behind new product releases. How often is the product updated and why? Is new product release market driven or engineering driven? What is the decision making process behind development priorities? Is it market or customer driven – in the sense that it delivers something better or cheaper – or is it engineering driven?

People

In acquisitions, where there is a high level of importance attached to technology, the orientation needs to be as much around people as products. If you are acquiring technology, you are acquiring people that you need to keep. Important questions are:

- Who is critical to the future, and why?
- How best to tie them in?

A related concern will be to find out who has is critical pieces of knowledge in their heads. How can this be best extracted? Who on the 'critical people' list and the 'undocumented critical knowledge' list is going to be dissatisfied by the deal or become very rich because of the deal?

The other people issue is the level of staffing in the areas vital for the technology's future performance. Are the development, testing and technical support teams adequately staffed? 'Adequate' includes both number and quality.

Conclusion

Technology due diligence is not just about assessing technical issues. Just as important are the people and the market issues. It is no good having the best mousetrap if the market for mousetraps is already saturated, if potential customers do not know of its existence or if they are not really bothered about upgrading. Similarly, a winning design now will soon be overwhelmed if the key technicians all leave – especially if they end up with the competition.

14 Intellectual property due diligence

Intellectual property is the intangible assets owned by the target that are protectable. It has four strands:

- Identification of the intellectual property rights (IPRs) in a business
- Ownership of those rights. As the IPRs necessary to carry on the business have to be transferred when the target is sold, a central concern of intellectual property due diligence is to establish that the seller owns the rights it is selling
- Validity. Once transferred, are those IPRs sufficient to protect the acquired company from claims that its activities are infringing the intellectual property rights of others?
- Uniqueness/sufficiency. Alongside the three more legal investigations outlined above, commercially you would be wise to satisfy yourself that the intellectual property you are buying is what you expect

How much to do

The first thing to note is that intellectual property rights vary by territory, including:

- The rights that are recognised
- How much and what sort of protection IPRs give
- How they are acquired and registered
- How, and for how long, they are maintained
- What constitutes an infringement
- Remedies available for infringements

Intellectual property due diligence should therefore take account of the laws in each relevant jurisdiction. But as it would be impossible for an investigation to cover all territories, local advice needs to be taken in those jurisdictions where there are significant sales or assets or where the business is going to be developed.

Where IP is relatively unimportant to the target's profitability, it might be enough merely to confirm that the IP rights are registered in the target's name and appear to be in good standing. Where the main asset is intellectual property, quite extensive enquiries might be required. These will go beyond verifying that the target company owns the intellectual property rights it says it owns to assessing their continuing worth to the business. This may well involve a close study of how easy it might be to engineer around patents and checking that there are no emerging technologies that might supplant them.

There may also be industry specific rights, and you will probably also want to include important items that are not intellectual property rights as such. These would include:

- Rights to use domain names
- Know how/trade secrets

Establishing ownership

It is important, first of all, to ensure that the seller has proper title. A company might not have proper title for a number of reasons:

- Employees' rights. In the UK, but not in all jurisdictions, if employees invent something during the normal course of their work, the rights to the invention are owned by their employer unless their contracts of employment state otherwise. If freelancers invent something in their normal course of employment, the intellectual property belongs to them unless there is an agreement that states otherwise. Designs belong to whoever commissioned them
- Group companies. It is not uncommon for several companies in a group to use rights that are owned and registered by only one of them. Intellectual property may have to be assigned or licenced as part of the deal if the target company is being sold out of a group
- Third party agreements. Title may also be affected by the terms on which technology has been licenced from third parties. In particular, the future of the target may be seriously undermined by:

  - Conditions limiting the right of the target to modify or adapt any licenced technology
  - Change of control clauses in the licencing agreement

It is therefore important to verify that all important rights are registered in the name of the target company or in the name of the company contracting to sell them. Software is an area of particular vulnerability because of the heavy use of freelance programmers.

It is possible that the seller may have encumbered the rights, and this needs to be checked out. With registered rights, the process is straightforward (at least in the UK). Encumbrances should be registered. If they are not, a purchaser buys the rights free of encumbrances. With unregistered IPRs, the opposite applies. The buyer will acquire encumbered assets, whether or not it knew of the encumbrances. It would be unwise, therefore, to rely exclusively on searches, and a purchaser should negotiate appropriate warranties as well.

The seller should also warrant the extent to which any employees have any rights for compensation related to the seller's IPRs. It is not unusual to find that employees are compensated in some way for the use of their inventions.

Establishing validity

There are six 'validity' questions:

- Are all patents owned by the target active? Are other rights registered?
- Do third parties have any rights in any jurisdictions in which you want to extend the target's operations?
- Can rights be registered in other jurisdictions?
- For both existing patents and patents pending, is the idea genuinely novel or is it likely to be challenged in the future?
- Have all maintenance fees been paid? If not, patents the target thought it had may have lapsed
- Are all the important licences adequate? This question can apply to licences granted and to licences given.

The seller should be asked to provide details of any infringement claims from third parties. The effects of losing intellectual property litigation can be terminal. For this reason, a very careful assessment needs to be made of any challenges to a company's intellectual property. Where there are infringement proceedings pending, an indemnity from the seller may not be good enough. If the other side wins, the target will not be able to sell its product in the territories where the action succeeds and is quite likely to suffer everywhere else too.

Whether, in the absence of claims, a buyer can assume that all is OK is very much a matter of judgement. Usually the most security a buyer will get is by making sure that core rights are registered in core jurisdictions. A seller would be very foolish indeed to warrant that registered intellectual property rights are valid. No examination of a patent's validity when it is registered can be fool proof and, given that (in the UK anyway) patents can be challenged until they expire, a claim could pop up at any time. With trademarks, there is very often no detailed examination, so again revocation proceedings could appear out of the blue.

Licences

Where the target is a licensee of intellectual property, the buyer needs to assess whether licences are adequate, bearing in mind that it may want the target and/or its technology to do new things and go to new places. Questions will include:

- Do the licences cover the right territories?
- Are rights sufficiently protected in those territories?
- Do the licences cover everything needed? It is not unusual for rights to be confined to a particular field of application
- Are there unacceptable restrictions? An obvious one is a restriction on the sale of competing products. The target may not have had competing products when it entered into the agreement, but the buyer might
- Do you understand and are you happy with the calculation of royalty payments (especially if there is a minimum)? Are you satisfied that royalty calculations cannot be manipulated? Do the royalty payments give/allow the target to make a reasonable return?
- Do the licences last long enough?
- Are there any conditions which would end the licence or its exclusivity? Minimum sales targets, for example?
- Is the licensor infringing on third party rights? As it will probably be impossible to verify that the licensor owns all the rights, an indemnity to cover third party infringement claims may be required
- Are there change of control clauses? If a licence is critical to a company's business, and if the licensor has the right to terminate the agreement on change of control, the buyer of the company needs the licensor's consent to a change of control before the deal is completed. If buying assets, then any licences would have to be assigned, and again there may be clauses which restrict assignment
- Are there likely to be any competition issues? An exclusive licence can have the effect of carving up a territory, and competition authorities do not approve of that sort of thing

Establishing uniqueness/sufficiency

The value of IPRs is the commercial benefits that they give. For this reason, the importance of the uniqueness/sufficiency issue cannot be overstressed. Its essence is whether intellectual property brings commercial advantages. This has two main strands:

- The extent of the commercial advantage brought by IPRs
- Whether this is likely to last:

  - Is anyone else achieving the same end without infringing the target's protected rights?
  - Can the protection be 'got round'?

A competitive edge may very well derive from uniqueness, but uniqueness in itself may not be enough. Registered rights might protect a unique product or process but if the competition can find a way of achieving the same ends without infringing those rights, intellectual property rights will not be sufficient to give an advantage.

The other side of the coin is what to do if the unique idea or product bring bought has not been protected? The answer is to assess how long it would take for a reasonably competent competitor to replicate it and then decide what to do as far as the deal is concerned.

Know how

Know how presents special problems as far as uniqueness is concerned. Know how can only be transferred by communication. Communication informs the buyer, but it does not 'disinform' the seller. It still 'knows how'. There has to be a non-compete covenant and the purchaser has to ensure that it will have access to all employees with 'know how' after the transaction is completed.

Conclusion

Intellectual property such as patents, know how, trademarks and copyright are important for differentiation through innovation and brand development. As a result, the proportion of companies' value made up of intellectual property can be huge. A buyer uses intellectual property due diligence to ensure that the intellectual property which it thinks it is buying exists, can be fully exploited and is going to bring the commercial benefits that have been assumed.

15 Anti-trust due diligence

There are three areas on which to focus:

* Merger control filings
* The risk of buying into anti-trust infringements
* The enforceability of the target's contracts because of anti-competitive clauses

Merger Control Filings

Pre- or post-merger filings are mandatory in many jurisdictions. A filing may be required in all countries where the target has assets or sales. The rules normally contain strict time limits with fines for lateness. In addition, sanctions for ignoring the rules can be severe. The sections below cover the salient points of EU, US and UK merger control. Systems in other jurisdictions tend to be based on the US or European systems, but there are a large number of variations. It is essential to take local advice.

EU merger control

In the EU, all 'concentrations' which have a 'Community dimension' must be notified to the European Commission. A 'concentration' occurs where one or more undertakings merge or acquire control of one or more other undertakings. A 'Community dimension' is where:

a   The combined total worldwide turnover of all the undertakings concerned is more than €2.5 billion
b   The combined aggregate turnover of all the undertakings is more than €100 million in each of at least three Member States
c   The aggregate turnover of each of at least two of the undertakings concerned is more than €25 million in each of the three Member States included in b) above

And

d   The aggregate Community-wide turnover of each of at least two of the undertakings concerned is more than €100 million

'Control' is defined as the possibility of exercising decisive influence. With this definition, even the purchase of a minority stake could be construed as control.

The 'concentration' may not be put into effect until the Commission clears the transaction. Failure to comply with this requirement can lead to fines of up to 10 per cent of the worldwide group turnover in all products and services of the corporate group involved.

The EU has introduced a one-stop shop approach for merger notification. This means that concentrations with a Community dimension must be notified only to the European Commission.

Concentrations that do not have a Community dimension might have to be notified to national authorities, depending on their filing requirements. The Commission can decide to refer concentrations with a Community dimension to national authorities under certain circumstances. Similarly, under certain circumstances national authorities can ask the Commission to review concentrations that do not have a Community dimension.

Getting clearance

Getting clearance is not an exact science. Combined market share is a basic measure and defining the market is crucial. The market test appears to be whether or not there are readily available and acceptable substitutes for the product in question. If a product is substitutable (as far as both consumers and producers are concerned), it cannot form its own product market.

The market share threshold which generates closer Commission scrutiny is around 40 per cent. At one end of the spectrum, a combined buyer/target market share of 25 per cent or less raises a presumption of no dominance. At the other end, a combined buyer/target market share of 50 per cent or more does the opposite. A market share of 70 per cent or higher can in itself constitute evidence of dominance.

'Collective dominance' is something else the Commission may look at. For example, in a mature market for an homogenous product, a small number of producers who collectively hold a market share in the range of 60 to 70 per cent or more may collectively dominate even though their individual shares are well below any of the normal thresholds. Collective dominance occurs when suppliers in a particular market do not compete but follow the behaviour of the market leader instead.

US anti-trust regulations (Hart-Scott-Rodino)

The 1976 Hart-Scott-Rodino Act (HSR) created a screening system at the Federal Trade Commission (FTC) and the Department of Justice (DOJ) so that mergers and acquisitions are reviewed before they happen. The test for lawfulness is similar to the European one: 'is the merger likely to substantially lessen competition?'

Basic requirements

Under HSR, all deals under $63 million are exempt from filing. All deals over $252 million must be filed. Transactions in between must be notified if the 'size of person' test is met.

The size of person test is usually met if one party has total assets or annual net sales of $126 million or more; and the other party has total assets or annual net sales of $12.6 million or more. For purposes of HSR, the appropriate entity for measuring size of person is not necessarily the party to the transaction, but its 'ultimate parent entity'.

These thresholds apply to mergers, acquisitions of securities, asset acquisitions and the formation of joint ventures, and they are measured *after* the transaction. In other words, even a small transaction could push the acquiring entity over one of the thresholds.

Where the parties and the transaction meet the appropriate tests, US law says that the acquisition cannot take place until:

•   Both parties have filed pre-merger reports with the Federal Trade Commission

And

•   The Department of Justice and the HSR waiting period(s) expire

The waiting periods for most transactions are 30 days after both parties file their initial pre-merger reports. If the government requests additional information, there is an additional waiting period of 30 days. The main exception is for cash tender offers where the waiting periods are reduced to 15 days after the initial response and 10 days if there is a second response. An early Termination of the waiting period can be requested and is frequently granted.

A worksheet, with guidelines, is available at the FTC website, www.ftc.gov/bc/hsr.

National merger control

If a deal is not trapped by European merger control, it could still fall foul of national regulations. The regulations vary by country. UK merger control is covered by the Enterprise Act 2002, as amended by the Enterprise and Regulatory Reform Act 2013.

The Competition and Markets Authority published its 'Mergers: Guidance on the CMA's jurisdiction and procedure' (CMA2) in April 2014. First, there must be a merger. This is defined as occurring when two or more enterprises 'cease to be distinct'. This arises either when they are brought under common ownership or control.

The expression 'control' need not mean holding over 50 per cent. Material influence is enough to constitute control.

For a merger to qualify for investigation, one of two tests must be satisfied:

- Market share. This is met if, as a result of the merger, the combined enterprise accounts for at least 25 per cent of the supply or acquisition of particular goods or services, either in the UK as a whole or in a substantial part of it
- Sales. This is satisfied if the target's UK turnover exceeds £70 million

The UK operates a voluntary notification regime, but the CMA does send enquiry letters where it considers that completion concerns may arise. It has significant powers to take so-called 'hold separate' measures to preserve its remedy options if it ultimately finds competition concerns.

There is nothing to stop an acquisition completing, but it could be investigated subsequently, raising the possibility of the CMA remedies. If a buyer wishes to avoid merger control risk, it should notify the transaction and wait for clearance. The Phase 1 review (initial examination) timetable is 40 working days, after which there will be either a clearance decision or a full investigation (Phase 2). The Phase 2 timetable is 24 weeks.

Anti-trust risk

The risks of buying into anti-competitive behaviour are real and potentially very expensive. Therefore, as well as dealing with merger control filings, there may be other anti-trust issues which need investigating prior to completion.

The possibility of rigged markets is one of the most difficult areas to investigate. It is a clandestine activity that top management, let alone in-house lawyers or external advisers, often know nothing about. The anti-trust violations to watch out for in particular are those which:

- Directly or indirectly fix purchase or selling prices or any trading conditions through:
  - Abuse of dominant position
  - Market sharing or price fixing arrangements with competitors
  - Resale price maintenance – a vertical arrangement under which a supplier requires a purchaser to resell goods at a certain price
- Limit or control production, marketing, technical development or investment
- Share sources of supply with competitors
- Share sensitive information with competitors. This would include sales figures, pricing policy, price lists, discount structures and dates when prices will be increased
- Apply dissimilar conditions to equivalent transactions
- Impose obligations which have nothing to do with a particular transaction, such as making it a condition that a customer for product A buys product B before it is supplied with A

The following need to be added to the list in EU transactions:

- Absolute territorial protection of exclusive distributors
- Export restrictions within the EU

Contact with competitors is usual. The question for due diligence is the nature of those contacts. Trade Association meetings are the most obvious source of potential exposure. Minutes of such meetings and any other Trade Association correspondence should, therefore, be the first port of call. However, the odds of finding anything written down are slim, and because of this, it is vital for the due diligence team to get out and talk to those people in the target who have contact with the competition. Sales and marketing and planning personnel would be top of the list. These are also the people who are most likely to generate incriminating internal documents, perhaps describing in exaggerated terms, for example, the actions that the company should take against price cutting dealers and the like. Employees in the planning department are a high risk group, as their market intelligence activities may bring them into contact with competitors and result in exchanges of information.

Any commercial relationships between the target and its competitors (for example, in supply, licencing or joint venture agreements) should also be examined, along with any side deals that go with them.

After carving up the market, trying to fix who can sell what at what price comes next on the investigation list. The due diligence investigators should look first at the termination of dealers. Within the EU, terminations or threats to terminate dealers because of their pricing or parallel importing or exporting practices, may give rise to substantial anti-trust exposure. In many jurisdictions, agreements with dealers to maintain their retail prices are a serious anti-trust infringement. In the EU, preventing customers from exporting the supplier's products to another EU member country is generally prohibited. A company cannot guarantee absolute territorial protection to a distributor, although it can require its exclusive distributor not to *actively* seek customers outside its territory. Many jurisdictions forbid efforts by suppliers to tie in customers, like in the example mentioned earlier, by making them purchase product B as a condition for their being able to purchase product A. In some jurisdictions, it may be prohibited for a supplier to discriminate among similarly situated customers; in others, this may be a violation of competition law only where the supplier is in a dominant position. The rules are different in different jurisdictions, and whoever is conducting the due diligence needs to be aware of this.

Non-competition restrictions are not always illegal. Where a business is sold, non-competition clauses are allowed for a period not longer than would be needed by a third party to set up a similar business.

If the due diligence review uncovers anti-trust law violations, the question is how to limit the buyer's exposure. Under EU competition law, a buyer may be liable under certain circumstances for infringements committed by the target before the acquisition if the target merges with or into the buyer. If the target continues to operate as a separate legal entity in the buyer's group after the acquisition, the target itself will remain liable for its prior infringement, unless the seller was itself a party to the infringement with the target, in which case the seller remains liable. Among the alternatives the buyer can consider are the following:

- Pulling the deal
- Adjusting the purchase price to compensate for the risk
- Obtaining an indemnity from the seller
- Stopping any infringements by the target immediately after the acquisition
- Establishing a clear compliance policy for the future

Enforceability of contracts

In the EU, the work does not end with finding and dealing with anti-trust exposure. Here there is an additional risk, in that an agreement that restricts competition cannot be enforced.

Parties would normally have to go to the Commission and seek formal exemption, in order for what could otherwise be deemed restrictive agreements not to be illegal, unless they fall under the 'block' exemptions. On top of these, the Commission's De Minimis Notice provides a safe harbour for agreements between undertakings which the Commission considers to have non-appreciable effects on competition.

If an agreement is not covered by a block exemption, parties can seek an individual exemption from the Commission. Needless to say, obtaining an individual exemption decision is time-consuming – it may take several years. As a consequence, most notifications result in the Commission issuing comfort letters. These are not legally binding, but serve as evidence of the Commission's view.

Conclusion

Merger control filing is an essential part of the due diligence process on bigger deals. Smaller deals may or may not be caught by national regulations, depending on whether they cause sufficient concentration to worry the national authorities. Competition filings are territorial, i.e. they must be considered for each jurisdiction where the buyer and target have operations and/or assets. For this reason, it pays to look at anti-trust filings early on the process. Forgetting to file or filing too late can be expensive and cause delay.

As well as merger control filings, anti-trust due diligence should be concerned with the possibility of buying into anti-competitive behaviour. Flouting competition laws can be very expensive, so again, it is a fundamental part of due diligence to try to identify as early as possible any specific areas to do with competition law which may be of concern and to determine whether the remedies needed are such that they make the transaction unattractive. Finally, the due diligence process should also seek to identify contracts that may be unenforceable because of anti-trust law.

Printed in the United States
by Baker & Taylor Publisher Services